Sweet Dreams, Story Catcher

A commemorative collection of *Portland* magazine essays by

BRIAN DOYLE

Edited and Prologue by Janna Lopez

University *of* Portland

First edition.

Project management and content curation by Janna Lopez, Magazine MakeOver
Project oversight and copy editing by University of Portland, Office of Marketing and Communications
Art direction and graphic design by Karen Gibson, Orange Creative Group
Watercolors and illustrations by Meg Harvey, Orange Creative Group
Printed by Premier

BRIAN DOYLE arrived at the University of Portland in 1991. As the new editor of *Portland* magazine, his task was to help redefine the narrative and identity of the school. It was a role he cherished for 25 years, until in 2017, at 60 years old, he tragically lost his fight with cancer. Under Brian's vision and guidance, *Portland* was ranked one of the best university magazines in the nation.

Faith and Catholicism were central to Brian's life and work as an editor and writer. He was raised in an Irish Catholic family in New York, attended University of Notre Dame, and wrote for *U.S. Catholic* and *Boston College Magazine* before coming West.

He dubbed himself a "story catcher," and his perceptions and words reached thousands of people around the world through numerous published works. This book is a collection of deeply personal essays Brian wrote for *Portland* magazine over two decades. This curated selection honors Brian's life experiences as a story catcher. Through these essays, he shared his value of education, his reverent faith, his affection for nature, his thirst for insight, and his contemplations about life and death, as a friend, husband, and father.

With gratitude to Brian for sharing his innermost thoughts, prayers, and ideas, we offer this commemorative gift to the world as a way of saying to our story catcher, not "goodbye," but "sweet dreams."

PROLOGUE

Brian Doyle dreams to reincarnate as a hawk or otter. But mostly an otter.
Through gratitude and mercy he weeps joyful resonance over the best life ever:
    a woman too cool for him deft with a paint brush,
    twin boys and a daughter whose whimsey ignite him like a firefly,
    parents he professes his luck to like, love and admire,
    brothers bearing wildness and a sister most sweet,
    a childhood adorned by basketballs, books, bugs and Godly beliefs,
    slathers of friends and colleagues and students and faculty, each unassumingly stitching and
        shearing devoted memories into his human expression of love and miracles,
    words, reflections, observations and lore about our flawed misdeeds and depths of forgiveness.

Brian Doyle's passing tears become ours.
And so goes the hope, may this collection provide comfort.

In our hearts we hear his beating,
in his captured stories he observes the stardust and cosmos,
the knowing and the finite.

He was and is of this earth
where no mind can ever master
the mystery of
grace,
or laughter,
or humility,
or sorrow,
over the brilliant lights who dim too soon.

Arriving

My daughter Lily is three weeks old today. She weighs eight pounds and is approximately the size of a salmon. To date she is a contemplative child, much given to staring at lamplight and gazing meditatively out the window. She rather enjoys being naked, which worries her father, and she relishes being fed, being held close to the chest, and being tightly wrapped in blankets adorned with clowns. At night she squeaks and hums for fear her parents will forget that she is there; during the days she either sleeps like a rock or regards her father with unadulterated astonishment. Unromantic observers say that Lily's dark blue eyes are opened wide to catch the reflected light from my spectacles. I prefer to think she is astounded that her father appears to be wearing a badger on his face.

I stare at her with astonishment, too, but my reasons are more complicated. I am amazed at the litany of miracles that compose her — her tiny efficient heart, her eyes like blue pools, her newly-minted mind. I am amazed that a child so small can guzzle so much milk. I am amazed that a truck delivers 90 diapers a week to my door, and that I am so profoundly grateful for those diapers.

But I am most amazed at Lily's sheer existence, her Lilyness, and I spend a good deal of time wondering where she came from. I know she came from my wife, because I was there for the prison break. I know she came from Boston, because that ancient cobbled city is where my wife and I were living ten months ago. But I don't actually know — really know — where the breath that became Lily came from, although I have my suspicions.

Myself, I come from the East. I was born in New York but found my way eventually to New England, where I lived for many years. I lived in four towns and on two islands. I unloaded egg trucks, ran a tiny newspaper, and wrote for a large magazine. In July I arrived in Oregon to succeed John Soisson as editor of this magazine; in October my daughter arrived.

We have arrived in a place of enormous beauty and promise, I tell my daughter. She opens her eyes wide at this, but says nothing. I suspect she is staring at the badger.

WHAT
WE
LEARN
ABOUT
LEARNING

The Brilliant Floor

There was a girl named Linda in my first-grade class, at Saint John Vianney School in New York. She was shy and tall. She sat in front of me in the first row. We sat in alphabetical order, so that Accopardo was first seat first row and Wyzkyski was fifth row last seat. It was easiest that way for Sister Marie. She was also shy and tall. She was calm and tender and firm and maybe twenty years old. Most of us were six years old but four of us were five. Linda and I were among the fives. The sixes looked down on us as soon as they discovered we were five. They discovered this within the first week of school, and after that there were the sixes and then there were the fives. Why that should matter is a puzzle, but it mattered.

One day, after a particularly turbulent recess in the playground during which all four of the fives had suffered some indignity from the sixes, we trooped back into our classroom. In Sister Marie's class you were expected to carry the detritus of your lunch back to your desk, so that she could be sure that you had indeed taken sustenance; but this day Sister noticed that Linda's lunchbox was empty. No sandwich wrapper, no cookie crumbs, no apple core. Sister inquired; Linda sat mute. Sister pressed, gently, leaning down to Linda at her tiny desk; Linda covered her face with her hands and wept. Sister realized that Linda had been robbed of her lunch by the sixes, and had not eaten at all, and had been humiliated by the theft, and was more humiliated now by public revelation, and Sister straightened up and stared at each of the sixes, her face unreadable but just as she began to speak, Linda sobbed even harder, and a rill of urine trickled from the back of her seat and pooled on the floor between the first and second rows.

For a moment there was a ruckus as some children shouted and leapt away from the pool but then Sister said *Silence! Seats!* very firmly indeed — not shouting, but so firmly that everyone sat down in silence — and then she appointed Meghan to lead Linda to the girls' room and then to the school nurse. Meghan held out her arm just like a gentleman does in old movies and Linda took her arm and they stepped over the puddle and left the room. You could hear Linda sobbing all the way down the hall.

The best reason we have schools, I think, is to learn things for which we do not have words or equations. All teachers admit that their students will remember very little, if anything, of the curriculum they were taught; in the end what teachers really do is offer context, manners of approach, and the subtle suggestion that a cheerful humility before all problems of every sort is the only way toward useful grapple, let alone solution. What teachers really teach, it seems to me, is not a subject, but ways to be; a poor teacher teaches one way, and a fine teacher teaches many, some of which may be, to your amazement and relief, ways for you, the student, to open, to navigate, perhaps to soar.

Sister Marie was a fine teacher. We sat silently for a long moment, after Linda left, and then Sister sent a boy to the boys' room and a girl to the girls' room to get all the paper towels they could carry. They came back with one million paper towels. Sister gave each one of the sixes a handful of towel and they mopped up the puddle, one by one, in alphabetical order, by rows, silently. When they were finished Sister handed each of the remaining fives a handful of towel also, and we also knelt and scrubbed the brilliant floor. No one said a word. The sixes then collected our paper towels and put them in the trash. A little while later Linda and Meghan came back and sat down and we started into arithmetic. I never forgot this lesson, and I would bet that no one there that day ever did either. I would bet the house on that.

Ice & God

The stubborn man who invented the University of Portland was born in Vermont and raised on farms in Wisconsin and Minnesota, and he noted himself that his cold and hardscrabble childhood, and education at the feet of a Scottish Anglican father and an Irish Catholic mother, had taught him mostly about ice and God. He decided to pursue the latter professionally and was ordained a priest. Soon thereafter his talents as pastor and manager of men in the north country caught the sharp eyes of his pope, who sent him headlong into the wet fir jungles of the Pacific Northwest, first as bishop of Vancouver Island and then, in 1898, as fourth archbishop of Portland.

Alexander Christie smoked cigars incessantly, rode his horse everywhere, and was by all accounts almighty fond of ships and boats, riding up and down the Willamette River as often as he could get a keel beneath his feet. Legendarily parsimonious, he ran the finances of the vast archdiocese from a single desk drawer in his chancery, or more often, as he was always astride a ship or a horse, from a wad of bills in his pocket, from which he would reluctantly peel escapees with a furious glare. Fond of children, he made hundreds of unscheduled visits to grade schools and school picnics; indeed, a man well ahead of his time when it came to motivation theory, he was not at all averse to unscheduled visits to any remote corner of his bailiwick, on the theory that a sudden archbishop saw more unvarnished truth than an expected one.

When Christie arrived in Oregon there was no college for Catholic boys, a fact which stuck in his craw. One summer day, according to legend, he was boating on the river when he saw, high atop a bluff over Swan Island, the empty hall that had for a few years contained a struggling Methodist university. This building and many acres of attendant farmland were soon in Christie's hands, and before the summer was out, he had shanghaied a motley faculty and opened the University.

The remarkable story of Christie's university has been and will continue to be told in many venues, but it is Christie's stunning inventiveness that I wish to account here — the sheer mind-boggling creativity of the man. He dreamed a college into existence in *weeks*, going from river reverie to opening bell in the time it takes the modern university to assemble a committee on committees.

Alexander Christie wanted a Catholic college in Oregon, and by God he made one, in the blink of an eye. He did not convene advisors, or form an exploratory committee, or conduct a market survey; he just did it, objections be damned, and from that vigorous act has come a Western university that has lived for a century, may well live many centuries more, and has startled hearts and heads in countless ways public and private. No small feat, that: so a prayer, as we end this inventive century, for a headstrong man who best knew ice and God, and the heartfelt hope that he is warm in the love of the latter.

The Bell

One morning eight men gather in a room. Six of them are Irish, one is Dutch, and the other is French. The chief of this clan is a priest and his right-hand man is a priest also. They are both Murphys. There's a doctor there and two missionaries, and a man who speaks fluent Greek, and a man who loves mathematics, the poor creature.

They wait patiently for something to happen.

Murphy, the chief, maybe tells them about how he was a parish priest last year until the local bishop dragooned him into being the president of a university that didn't technically exactly actually exist on the day he was named president.

They grin and wait.

Murphy the right-hand man suggests they review their prospective duties.

Good on you, Jim, says the chief. I'll go first. I'll teach religion.

All religions? says one of the eager young fellas, O'Leary maybe or O'Farrell, you can't tell them apart.

There's only the one true religion, lad, says the chief. We'll teach that one.

Murphy the right-hand man will teach literature and grammar and Latin and Greek, in which he is fluent, not that there's much call for fluent Greek conversation here on the edge of the vast forest.

Sullivan, the dean, will teach law and bookkeeping.

Aloysius Reidhaar, who indeed does have red hair, will teach the four languages in which he is fluent: Italian, Spanish, German, and French.

Arthur DeLorimier, the Frenchman, will teach science and mathematics, which he loves, the poor thing.

O'Farrell and O'Leary, the eager young seminarians, will teach everything else, and Andrew Smith, the doctor, will be the doctor.

All right, then, says the chief. Any other business at hand? No one speaks.

They hear the voices of boys outside the windows. A dozen boys maybe, their voices scattered by the wind off the river. It's early September, still high summer here although the nights are crisp, and the boys are, in the way of all boys everywhere forever, rambling and tussling and teasing and wrassling when they are supposed to be gathering in orderly fashion on the steps of the hall where the eight men are meeting.

There are a few boys out there, chief, says Sullivan. Should we start, do you think?

I guess so, says Murphy. Ring the bell.

That bell rang at "about ten in the morning," say the annals of the University of Portland casually, and when its peal rang out across the steps of what was then West Hall, and out through the lanky fir trees that once graced the bluff, and upriver toward the steaming city, and downriver toward the roaring sawmills, and east toward the sweating ranches of the sage-lands, something began that had never been in the world before.

That thing turned one hundred years old on September 5. It's a grand thing now, populous, almost famous, sure of itself, no longer scrawny and scrabbling though still lean and hungry, and since that summer morning in 1901 some thirty thousand men and women have lived and worked and studied here, and the university that began that morning has now sparked hearts for a century in ways no one can ever calculate, not even Arthur DeLorimier, who so loved mathematics, the poor soul.

That's why many people love it dearly, including, with great respect and rich affection, me.

Bruised with Joy

I have been typing furiously on behalf of the University of Portland for twenty years, which is a hilarious and terrifying sentence for all sorts of reasons, but after some four thousand days on The Bluff, I find myself more absorbed than ever before. How could that be? Is this not when I should grow weary and cynical about the corporation, and shriek at the shocking price tag for the product, and note testily that you cannot even define the product, except with such ephemeral gossamer murk as *epiphany* or *awakening* or *shiver of the heart*?

And yet, try as I might, I cannot achieve a healthy skepticism. For one thing I keep meeting the kids here, the endless river of lanky gracious generous verbs who sizzle your heart every time you talk to them; if theirs are the (enormous) hands which will soon run the world, what a lovely world it will be, I keep thinking. And then there are so many cheerful nuts among the staff and faculty and alumni and donors who insist that this place *matters* in mysterious ways, that there is no place like it in the world, that some odd combination of passion and poetry and vigor and vision opens miraculous doors in our students, doors through which their extraordinary gifts come pouring out and the ocean of complicated grace pours in, doors that perhaps never would have been opened without their years here.

And also without fail every time I slough toward despond a story comes and thrums on my heart until I am bruised with joy. I see a child's face when the best soccer player in America shakes her hand and asks her about *her* world. I see the face of a man who survived seven hells in the war as he tells me huddled in a sandy hole thinking of his professors here, *they'd have been after me to use my foxhole time to practice my Latin,* he says, grinning. I see the face of my late friend Becky Houck, who when I asked her how in heaven's name she could possibly stay in her office until midnight talking to frightened freshmen every night, said, with real surprise, *why, they're all my children, of course, wouldn't you do that for your children?*

And I read the letter I received one day years ago from a woman never to be named. There had been an essay in this magazine, she wrote, that broke her and opened her, and she was writing to tell me about it, because I should know that a door in her heart had opened, and it would never be closed again, not ever, and this magazine and this university threw it open, and she had cried and cried, and then sat down to write this letter with a pen she found in the kitchen drawer. God had given her a son, she wrote, and her boy was blind and deaf and crippled, and he had never even sat up, let alone walked, and soon he died, and her heart was so torn and shredded that she locked up his memory and hid it away, for years and years, but then this magazine came and thrummed on her heart, and she began to cry, and remembered a moment when she was bathing him, and a bar of sunlight hit his face, and he turned into the light as he felt the light caress him, and he smiled and laughed at the kiss of the light, and she had not thought of that moment in years and years, and now she would never forget it ever again.

The University did that. This university does that a thousand times a day in ways we'll never know. When I have dark days, when I have days I think the University of Portland is a muddled corporation no different than a thousand other colleges, when I have days I shriek at the cost, and snarl with fury at all the kids who should be here and can't afford it, I think of that letter. We did that. We open the most stunning doors, through which the most stunning light gets in and out. No one can count the number and nature of the doors we open. Isn't that great?

One Night

The coolest thing about the University of Portland story is that there isn't one — there are zillions, some of which are hilarious, like the gentlemanly land scam idea the founders had for paying for the new place, or the time the University president traded the bull that serviced local cows for a new Studebaker, and some are haunting, like the time a University president had a heart attack and died on the stage at Howard Hall, or the boy ninety years ago who moved into his dorm room and then dove in the river and never emerged, and some are hilarious but tense, like a new vice president forty years ago discovering that we were technically bankrupt and his official first phone call is begging to the bank, and some are sweet and nutty, like the way the women's soccer team used to wander up into the stands barefoot after a game to shake hands with every kid who wanted to shake hands and get autographs, and then there are some stories that make you shiver and pray, like this one.

Recently I sat in a little chapel filled with one hundred boys upon whom unimaginable crimes and sins had been committed, boys who had endured and survived more species of pain and desolation than I could account in a year, boys who had been married to sadness for years, boys who were thrashing all day every day toward some kind of shivering peace and rebirth, and every other one of these boys was bouncing his feet, or nodding his head, or grinning widely, or snapping his fingers, because there was a University of Portland alumnus standing where the altar usually is, and he was singing and roaring, and banging away beautifully on his enormous guitar, and the wild deft musicians behind him were making a muscle of music so joyous and fast and captivating that you just could not sit still, no matter how cool you wanted to seem, or how deep inside yourself you crouched as protection against rage and pain and fire, and the boy in front of me was rocking and bouncing like he was about to launch into space, and then he burst into tears, and he cried for the rest of the hour, although he never stopped rocking and bouncing for an instant. I watched his tears slide down his face into his suit jacket, which was hairy and too small for him, and I wondered how many tears had been wept into that jacket, but there is no way to tell.

At the end of the concert, when the band had finished with an incredible flourish and it was okay for everyone to jump up and yell, the boy shot out of his chair and jumped up and down laughing until finally he and everyone else settled down to a dull roar and began to pile out of the pews. Then every single boy in the chapel went up to the members of the band and shook their hands and said *thank you, sir*, and then they lined up in barrack order and walked out of the chapel rustling and humming.

I saw this. I was there. I'll never forget that boy. Something hit his heart right amidships, right in the place where joy and hope were down to their last lost grains, and it was a University of Portland man who delivered that thrilling blow, and I saw it delivered, and I saw it land. That's what the University of Portland is for, hitting kids in the heart. It happens all the time. It happens in a zillion ways. I saw one way, one night, and I'll never forget it.

In the Country of Poetry

The best teacher I know is a small man named Francis. He is a brilliant and disheveled man much given to poetry, which issues from him in thick sudden snatches. A talk about rabbits brings forth a rich burst of Blake; politics produces Auden, dry and angry; a casual remark about glowering weather draws forth the marching orotundity of Wordsworth. Sometimes, late in the afternoon, Francis will quietly quote from his own poems, which fill several books. His tongue handles his own lines with the stern affection of a father.

For nearly 50 years Francis has taught literature to college freshmen, whom he calls unscrambled eggs. I suspect his attachment to freshmen is due in part to the fact that they have no idea who he is. He is a shy man. They do not know, on that first day of class, when they find their seats and open their crisp new notebooks and see a small man with beans spilled on his tie, that he is a priest, that his friend Tom was better known as T.S. Eliot, that his friend Seamus is the poet laureate of Ireland, that he has written things that make people sob, that his heart

gave out when he was young and was rebuilt on an operating table and that he woke up expecting to be dead.

I've never seen him teach; he forbids visitors to his classroom, because he believes that both teaching and learning are private acts. But once, I am ashamed to say, I could not refrain from walking by the door of his classroom and snatching a glance at his class in progress. It was spring and the door was flung open. I could hear Francis clearly — he was chanting some lines from Blake, which hung in the air like herons — but all I could see, in that passing instant, was the rapt face of an enormous boy who had taken refuge in the very last row of the old classroom. Though seated where dawdlers and dreamers sit, he neither dawdled nor dreamed; he was engrossed, and he leaned forward on his elbows, straining to catch the velvet mumble of the elderly poet before him.

Teaching is exuberance and wit, humor and rigor, a sacrifice and a gift. It is the face of a boy in the country of poetry, and the rich song of his teacher spilling his heart in the air.

Some Things

That I have noticed here at the University over the past twenty years, things that give me the joyful willies, tiny things that are not tiny at all in the least whatsoever: the way the women's soccer team took their shoes and socks off after yet another victory, and sat in a cheerful ragged circle on the sweet moist field, and then wandered up into the stands to sit with children and shake their startled hands and sign tickets and jackets and shirts and hands and one tiny forehead, whose owner beamed like the sun. The way some tall shy lean children here walk around in their Army and Air Force uniforms on Tuesdays, uncomfortable and proud and scared and proud. The way sandhill cranes float over campus in October, so high up you can hardly see them, although you can hear their dark basso gurgling *quarwk*, and the way people who hear them will touch passersby on the elbows and say *hey, listen, cranes!* The way students say *hey, Father* when a priest ambles by, and the priest, no matter which priest he happens to be, almost always knows the long child by his or her first name, isn't that amazing? The way the wind shifts around during the day and what was the seethe of cedar in the morning becomes the whew of industrial paint from the vast roiling shipyards below the bluff. The way you can almost always find one person young or old weeping quietly in the dark in the back of the chapel, near the Madonna. The way water burbles in the chapel all day all night ever since the day the chapel opened its new huge walnut doors as big as bears. The way alumni at reunion seize each other by the hand with actual no kidding ferocious glee and shake hands much longer than the usual business deal. The way the bell tower startles visitors who did not know the tower spoke so boomingly and ringingly. The whir of golf carts carrying older priests hither and yon. The wealth of orders of nuns who grace the place. The way ballboys at basketball games sprint out bravely into the thicket of lank and burl to mop the floor where a muscled hero fell a moment before. The way the baseball coach grins at comic remarks offered by the folks in the rain in the wooden bleachers, and how there is always a cigar going somewhere in the stands even though there is Absolutely No Smoking whatsoever. The way a solid shot to right field occasionally hits Corrado Hall smack in the eastern shoulder with a resounding *crack!* and the way the hall sneers and rolls the ball back toward the field. The sound that foul balls make when they land with a *crunk!* on the hoods of cars parked near the baseball field. The milling of grinning graduates in leis and serapes and bright scarves just after graduation and the way the dense crowd of graduates and families and friends calves here and there into hilarious photo opportunities. The whirl of hawks and eagles in mating dances high over campus in spring. The way you can see the flicker of the huge fireplace in the Commons from way across the quad at night and it looks wonderfully warm and friendly and gentle and alluring and when you walk through the door and turn toward the fireplace someone says *hey come sit with us!* and you do, and somehow that's not a little thing, that's a huge thing, and somehow that matters deeply, and somehow that *is* the University, in ways that I cannot explain very well, hard as I try.

STUNNING
AND
LOVELY

The Loquacious Man

I have been a Catholic since 1956, when I was baptized wearing a white dress. My forebears, family, friends, schools, and employers were Catholic. Catholicism was my language, my coat, my house. I learned to pray in two American Catholic tongues, Latin and English, and to relish the smoky poetry of the Mass, an ancient ritual prayer. I chanted the Rosary with my brothers and sister, I prayed to St. Francis when I found the huddled corpses of sparrows, I prayed to St. Blase when my throat burned. When I was 12 my grandmother shriveled and died and I prayed desperately for her soul during her funeral Mass, a sad waltz which taught me the enormous power of ritual, the skeleton that sustains us when we are weak.

Then I stopped praying. It seemed pointless, a speech delivered to an empty room, a plea without ears. Many years passed. I grew up. Slowly I began to hear and see and taste prayers: a fox against snow, my wife's hand, my mother's corduroy voice. One morning on an island I went to get my mail and two purple finches flew out of the mailbox and I knew that they were prayers. One day, years later, a cold doctor said to me You will never have children, and that night I opened my mouth and prayed to the woods and skies and birds, to the shambling God I could not find but sensed everywhere, and since that day I have prayed silently and aloud, with my hands and feet, with my heart.

It seems to me now that all things are prayers. Curiosity and memory and silence and water are prayers. People are prayers. I have a daughter now, two years old, an exuberant prayer. We talk about God, whom she calls Gott. When she is asleep my wife and I cover her with one blanket and two prayers.

As a boy I learned the names of the boxes that prayers were mailed in: Our Father, Hail Mary, the Mass of the Dead. I came to hate the boxes because they seemed empty. I did not see that they were a means to an end, and that the end was a piercing conversation with Gott, the man who is nowhere and everywhere, who is not a man, who was a man, who never stops talking.

Stunning & Lovely

When I was a child, many years ago, at a parish named for a saint famous for hearing confessions eighteen hours at a pop, my life was graced by Dominican nuns, some of whom had ropy forearms like stevedores, and by Franciscan monks, all of whom seemed to have knotted feet made from tree roots, and once by a Jesuit, who looked so forbiddingly intelligent that we schoolchildren scattered like sparrows when he passed silently through the schoolyard, because rumor had it that Jesuits had laser eyes and could kill sparrows by staring at them hard, but most of us thought this was silly, although all of us flittered away from the Jesuit right quick, I noticed.

Thus I was introduced, when young, to the different flavors of Catholic charism — the Order of Preachers in their brilliant whites, the Order of Friars Minor in their quiet browns, and the brainy blackrobed intensity of the Society of Jesus, not to mention the steady priests of the Archdiocese of New York, who generally dressed like dentists on golf outings when they weren't in uniform. The religious orders, it seemed to us boys, were not unlike the military, with Regular Army personnel carrying most of the daily duty and specialists coming in for specific tasks — the Franciscans to conduct retreats, the Jesuit for astrophysics seminars or other such incomprehensible rites, the burly Dominican sisters to haul our faltering mental machinery into the shop for heroic renovation and repair. Not until I got to college, where I encountered the cheerful men of the Congregation of Holy Cross and their nutty insistence that I could learn as much or more outside the classroom than in, and to middle age, when I became absorbed by the Sisters of the Holy Names of Jesus and Mary and their nutty insistence that missionary work was as crucial Here as There, did I begin to pay close attention to the infinitesimal but riveting distinctions among the Catholic orders.

In a real sense the military model holds water still, for it seems to me that the Catholic orders, like the various services, are agents finally of peace; and the Catholic orders are all adamant ambassadors of the same brave hope and crazy conviction, that life defeats death, hope defeats despair, light defeats dark; they're all on the same team, as it were. Yet each comes at the mountain of problems along a slightly different path. Work is prayer, say the Benedictines, insisting that actions are more eloquent than words. Epiphany is *everywhere* available, say the Holy Cross men and women, and an education of the heart is as crucial as that of the mind. In the beginning was the Word, say the Order of Preachers, and the Word is God, and we will speak the Word wide. We are all brothers and sisters in the Love, say the Franciscans, who insist on living the gospel, not just analyzing it — if *necessary* use words, as their entertaining founder noted. Go thou to *the most difficult and extreme fields,* said Pope Paul VI to the Jesuits, and away they still go, agents of love into the jungles of despair, examples to their students of quiet courage changing the world. And there are as many more examples as there are Catholic orders in higher education; but for all the thrashing about that we poor badgers in their sales offices must do, trying to shout the differences among them so as to secure market share, I confess here that in our hearts we are thrilled that the differences are so tiny — shimmers of sunlight, really. Every color in the rainbow wears a different jacket, but the colors together compose something stunning and lovely beyond words, yes?

Two Hearts

Some months ago my wife delivered twin sons one minute apart. The older is Joseph and the younger is Liam. Joseph is dark and Liam is light. Joseph is healthy and Liam is not. Joseph has a whole heart and Liam has half. This means that Liam will have two major surgeries before he is three years old. The first surgery — during which a doctor will slice open my son's chest with a razor, saw his breastbone in half, and reconstruct the flawed plumbing of his heart — is imminent.

I have read many pamphlets about Liam's problem. I have watched many doctors' hands drawing red and blue lines on pieces of white paper. They are trying to show me why Liam's heart doesn't work properly. Blue lines are for blood that needs oxygen. Red lines are for blood that needs to be pumped out of the heart. I watch the markers in the doctors' hands. Here comes red, there goes blue. The heart is a railroad station where the trains are switched to different tracks. A normal heart switches trains flawlessly two billion times in a life; in an abnormal heart, like Liam's, the trains crash and the station crumbles to dust.

There are many nights just now when I tuck Liam and his wheezing train station under my beard in the blue night hours and think about his Maker. I would kill the god who sentenced him to such awful pain, I would stab Him in the heart like He stabbed my son, I would shove my fury in His face like a fist, but I know in my own broken heart that this same god made my magic boys, shaped their apple faces and coyote eyes, put joy in the eager suck of their mouths. So it is that my hands are clenched not in anger but in confused and merry and bitter prayer.

I talk to God more than I admit. Why did you break my boy? I ask. I gave you that boy, He says, and his lean brown brother, and the elfin daughter you love so. But you wrote death on his heart, I say. I write death on all hearts, He says, just as I write life. This is where our conversation always ends, and I am left holding the extraordinary awful perfect prayer of my second son, who snores like a seal, who might die tomorrow, who did not die today.

The Genius of It

Let's focus on the genius of Catholicism, which is the fact that it is illogical, unreasonable, unthinkable, unprovable, nonsensical, countercultural, and in direct defiance of all evidence and human history. Isn't that great? Isn't the loopiness at the center of it the best thing of all? We never admit that — but maybe we should celebrate it. Could it be that the wildness of it is the ring of truth?

Let me get this straight: the very essence of our common belief, the polestar by which we steer our lives, is the fact that a thin young Jewish man two thousand years ago insisted that life defeats death, hope defeats despair, light defeats darkness? That's ridiculous. That's silly. The evidence is everywhere against it. But He insisted on it, to the point of death — and whether you believe He rose from the dead and again walked the earth for three days, asking for something to eat, or you do not believe such a tall tale, the inarguable fact is that his insistence, his story, his wild message, has persisted and persisted and persisted. Why? It's not only the religious structure built atop his message that helped his voice persist into our time — I believe it is His insistence on that which is wholly unreasonable that touches us deepest in our hearts, that reaches down and makes us shiver in our deepest bones that rings the deep bell of truth inside us all. I believe His message and His genius has persisted because it is finally about hope and about the deepest feelings we have as human animals — feelings so deep inside us that they burst out only occasionally, and are often terrifying and rattling when they erupt. Because hope flies in the face of every shred of evidence, I believe in it. Isn't that wonderful? Isn't belief that hope defeats despair a wild leap like the ones we take when we commit to marriage, to a vocation, to a tumultuous democracy? Isn't it foolish to believe in light and life, given all the evidence against? But doesn't being foolish feel altogether right, in every cell of your body? Wouldn't a testy insistence on believing only that which you can see and touch and smell seem finally like a defeat, like a retreat, like a loneliness?

Let's focus on the Americanness of American Catholicism — the odd sweet mix of thorny prickly independence and warm brave thorough communal fabric that is this country. Let's look at Catholicism for a moment through the American lens, and see what happened to it here, on what many of the first people here called Turtle Island, on this rich new continent, in this utterly unique national idea — what happened to an ancient religion when it became the blood and breath and song and hope of people here? Maybe American Catholics like Annie Dillard and Andre Dubus

and Joseph Bernardin, all of whom were respectful of the past but looking past and through it — maybe they are dreamers of the future reality — as Christ and Gandhi and Tutu were and are dreamers of the substance of things hoped for. For many years Catholicism simply fought for its life in this land, fought to exist, fought not to be crushed. But now that we are established, that there are sixty million American Catholics and more coming every day, now that Catholic colleges and universities have become more and more the factories that produce the most eager, curious, selfless young Catholics, now that Catholic colleges and universities have risen ever higher in national prominence and voice, now that Catholic artists like Flannery O'Connor and Bruce Springsteen have been acclaimed among the best in American history — now what? Might the story of American Catholicism now be less insisting on the rights of Catholic Americans than insisting on the heights of American Catholics? *What now will we be?* How can we elevate and energize and shove and rebuild and resurrect the Catholic idea here? How can we push past the occasional inarguable cruelty and lies of our faith in practice, and practice far more what we know to be the bony simple charge at the heart of it, to feed the hungry, clothe the naked, comfort the lonely and broken, bring healing and hope to bear as the most brilliant weapons of all?

Sometimes I wonder if we realize how extraordinarily crucial Catholic universities are. They are the advance scouts of Catholicism to come, perhaps, the heights from which we see new country ahead. We American Catholics are of the old Church, of the Old World, as we are of Judaism, of the root stock, but in both cases we have forged on ahead. The old battles are fought and won, and we are free to go…where? Could it be that American Catholics, having been seared with fury over rape and crime among us, will emerge from the ash to shape the energy of the young into a faith that carries hope and healing into millions more hearts? That finds ways to heal rifts among the vast Christian tribes? That finds cousinship with Islam, which also bows to the One and to the Madonna? The faith we were raised in has passed — what is the faith in which our children will raise their children?

Let's focus on the ocean beneath the boat, as it were, because you know and I know that religions are boats on a far greater ocean. Deep beneath the religion is something so humanly true, so shiveringly possible, that I am convinced American Catholicism points to the riveting future that may be born. Think, for example, of a Catholic university not as a stalwart outpost of the Catholic Church that is, but as an advance guard for the Catholicism that may be. Think of the university's students not as scholars of theology and religion but as scouts for how Catholicism might continue to morph and grow and burrow deeper into all hearts. Remember how many kids go through Catholic universities and are changed in their deepest beings. We do not convert them to Catholicism so much as they see Catholicism at work in hearts and heads and hands; that is the greatness of the Catholic university, and the brilliance of the subtlety in faith formation. We present the unreasonable, show it in action every hour of every day, leave our students to gape in amazement, and prompt them to wonder how they can bring *their* gifts to bear…

Let's think for an evening not of Catholicism the religion, but Catholicism the genius idea — an idea that has everything to do with relentless unquenchable irresistible crazy insistent hope. It may be that the human capacity to hope, to dream what might be, to have visions, is finally the reason we are here, the reason we evolved to this point, and our greatest responsibility as creatures of the Lord. Some questions, then, for us to chew on: Could it be that our greatest talent and tool and skill is the ability to insist on the illogical and unreasonable, and so force the holy peace of the future into being? Could we be the means by which the future will be born? Could the Christ in us be the greatest evolutionary tool of all? Could our deep crazy insistence that everything is miraculous and soaked in holiness be the very means by which human beings finally achieve what the Creator hoped against all evidence that we might achieve? Could our utterly unreasonable faith that human beings can rise to astonishing grace and courage and creativity be the very reason that we are given free will with which to crash or soar? Could our genius for hope be the only tool that in the end defeats suffering? Could our absolute conviction that the thin Jewish man long ago was right when He insisted that hope defeats despair, life defeats death, light defeats darkness be the road that carries all of humanity past its addiction to violence? Could the secret be not Resurrection of one man, but Resurrection of a whole species of beings? Could the secret to a world of peace and laughter be not Christ alone, but Christ rising in each of us? Could Christ-in-us be a far vaster idea and gift than merely for Christians? Could Christ-in-us be the secret to all religions? Could Christ-in-us be the reason human beings were lifted from the other species of living beings, and given the gifts of sadness and reflection, mysticism and vision, hilarity and art, brains with unplumbed depths? Could Christ-in-us, the divine splinter slammed

into every heart, be what we are here for? Could that be why His story is so persistent and insistent and mysterious and uneasy? Could His story be far bigger, bigger than any religion?

So much of religion is mere cultural drape and accident — but spirituality is pan-cultural. We are all haunted as spiritual beings struggling for words to clothe the unimaginable but undeniable. We all know full well deep in our hearts that which is holy and that which is evil. We know what is love and what is sham. We know that religions are only languages and vocabularies and symbol systems for us to use as grappling hooks — they are lovely languages, and no one loves the redolent mythic brilliant magic and ritual and succor of Catholicism more than me. But it is a small house in a universe of mansions. There are many mansions in my Father's house…

Yet it seems to me that Catholicism, and especially American Catholicism, catches at more of the deep human spiritual genius than any other faith. Judaism and Islam are finally abject worship of the all-powerful One, and brilliantly designed systems for living in a tumultuous world where all are weak; Hinduism seems to me a dense lovely ancient seething grappling with all the energies and forces of the world, a wondrously tendrilled attempt to name them, put faces to them, ascribe them powers, make of them entities to entreat; Buddhism, though closest to Catholicism in its insistence that attentiveness is the door to holiness, also a panoply of sacred energies and powers; but Catholicism seems far more joyous, far more celebratory, far more invitation to partnership, far more expectation of responsibility in creating the wonder of the future than mere acceptance of the Mastery. We worship the One, from Whom all things come, but we savor the genius of the Son, who is us. That is the point. That is the brilliance. That is the genius. It isn't that He rose once — it's that He rises again and again and again and again day after day city after city soul after soul, again and again and again, unstoppable, irresistible, miraculous every moment. Catholicism is not Master and Servant — it is Father asking children to rise to their best selves, to accept responsibility, to use their holy tools to create what can be. In a real sense we as nominal adults are merely hoary older teenagers, with all the glorious energy and creativity and possibility of a teenager, as well as all the selfishness and blindness and self-absorption and laziness and disorganization. All is not ordained, all is not already created; from the tools we have been given, the incredible one-in-ten-billion-years tools each of us is given, *we* are asked to help create. We are asked to be Artists! What a gift! What a joy! What an astonishing and terrifying assignment!

And deep deep deep down in the bones of Catholicism there is a wisdom beyond words. You know and I know that there is so much more going on than ever we could see, could sense, could identify, could struggle to name. We know there are worlds beyond worlds, this is the great energy of our sciences, that we discover and discover and we never come to the end of discovery; if we think this to be true of the physical universe itself, can we think it is not true of all aspects of the universe? And again we struggle for words to describe what we know to be true but cannot articulate — visions and hallucinations, voices and signs, interventions and miracles… It is unreasonable to believe, illogical, nonsensical — but it seems to me impossible finally *not* to believe. To believe only in your senses — is that selfish? Is that a function of fear? Is the intellect the only door?

Let me make this discussion bluntly real. Where is the great beloved biology professor Becky Houck, who died last summer? Where is the Becky Houckness of Becky Houck? We know the principles of physics in this particular universe, though there may be many others — all things dissolve, and no energy is lost. And we know of the vessel that was the extraordinary teacher Becky Houck, the halo of hair and the beaming grin, the famous ballet slippers and the sweater as big as a coat, that quick bright intelligent voice, the slip of a body that once was the high school prom queen — gone, dissolved, returned to the dust and salt and water from which it came. But the electricity that *is* Becky Houck — the zest and verve, the laughter and kindness, the wit and generosity, the verb of her personality, the bone of her character — can anyone be absolutely sure that it has died? Are your senses so very accurate that you can say she is not traveling further than we can ever imagine? And I mean this far beyond the tropes we use — that her memory will never die, that her spirit is in the bricks of the halls she graced, that while we rememberher and speak of her she cannot die utterly — I mean it very literally

indeed. I believe she *is*, in ways and means and forms and shapes we will never know, and can only invent childish image for. I believe she lives. Out of the darkness she has danced into the light. Someone will say, but we do not understand how that can be! To which I reply cheerfully, me neither! So what!

It comes down to hope. That is the food of this nation and this religion. That is the great song of the human being. It doesn't make sense. But again and again we do not make sense in every conceivable arena and again and again we punch through sense and reason and logic into the far deeper ocean for which the only word that applies is love — a love nearly beyond our ken — but not quite. The genius of Catholicism is that *Christ is us* — inside each of us is the extraordinary key to the substance of things hoped for. The genius of Americanness is independence married to responsibility. Here, in America, we are free to reach for the stars, to create anything we can dream, to hold hands with our fellows and leap for the light. Here, in America, Catholicism may surge forward into a new rich wild creativity that opens yet another door toward who we might finally be, if we drop our weapons, and remove the beams from our eyes, and mill our extraordinary gifts into the fabric of a world where no child weeps, no child is terrified, wars are a memory, and we eat wonder all day like the most amazing and nutritious food.

It *can* happen, you know, and if it happens I think that it may happen here. There was never a national idea like America, and for all the violence and greed of our history there is still no idea as brave and wild and nonsensical and brilliant and generous as America. There was never an idea like Catholicism, and for all the violence and greed of that far longer story, there is still no idea as brave and wild and unreasonable and generous at its heart. What if the wildest national idea and the wildest religious idea kept going and growing and influencing each other and sending out new brilliant agents of hope in the future from campuses like this one? What might happen then? Now that America and Catholicism are married, what will be their sweet wild child?

An Ancient Promise

My friend Thomas became a priest when he was 28 years old. Before he donned the Crow Suit, as he calls his cassock, he was a physical therapist who had a sweet Southern girlfriend. One summer day he packed his old car with his gear and drove to a seminary. Five years later he was an assistant pastor in a Memphis slum. Since then he's served stints in parishes in Chicago and New York; today, at age 36, he is the chaplain of a New York hospital.

He is on call 24 hours a day and his face shows it. There are gray hairs in his beard and he smokes two packs of cigarettes a day. He lives in two rooms with two birds. He is at the same time the most direct and the most gentle man I know. He has been at the bedside of dying children more times than he can remember.

"What do you tell them?" I asked.

"That God will hold them in his hands," he said.

"How can you stand it?" I asked.

"Somebody has to take care of their souls."

A few months after he packed his car and drove to the seminary we were drinking old whiskey together on Christmas Eve, a tradition we adhered to for many years. We met every year in a bar under a railroad track. When a freight went over the bottles jumped and startled behind the bar; sometimes the jukebox would shut itself off.

"Why do you want to be a priest?" I asked.

"Because my guts said so."

"What the hell does that mean?"

"I don't know, Brian," said Tom patiently. "I just know this is what I should do. I believe that people have souls, and that their souls are eternal, and that what they do on earth matters enormously. I believe that there are men and women who give up one life to help people with that other life, and I think I'm one of those men. I never cared much for the formal Church, for the politics and rituals and regulations, but there is something deep in the priesthood, something inarticulate, something that stabs me in the heart. You can't dress it up in words because words fall off it. It's ancient and holy. Let's drink to it."

I did and I do.

A Thin Ragged Man

Several months ago a man named Walter appeared at our door. He was a slight ragged man, gaunt, dirty, polite. He worked hard all day in the basement, sheet-rocking walls and building a wooden floor. He worked hard all the next day too. The third day he barely worked at all. He spent the day eating sandwiches and talking about himself. He had served three tours in Vietnam, some of them in a psychiatric ward. He said that he had a wife and child but they left him, that someone had recently stolen his truck and tools, that he was grateful for the work in our basement.

On the first day he had estimated the cost of his work and we agreed on a price. I bought all the supplies and borrowed tools. On the second day he asked for an advance and got it. On the third day he asked for another advance and got it. He also asked for a raincoat and a ride into the city and got them too. I dropped him off in the city; my daughter and I waved to him as he shuffled off.

That was the last we saw of Walter for a while. I returned the tools. Two weeks later he showed up and worked hard all day again. He said he'd badly underbid the job and asked for another advance. We said no. His face fell. He was out on the streets, he said, and needed to find ten dollars a day for his methadone shot. We said no. He saw my wife's beloved old backpack and sleeping bag and proposed that he finish the job in exchange for them. Okay, said my wife. And Walter walked off into a howling thunderstorm carrying the pack and bag and we never saw him again.

Walter is a thief, a hapless ragged polite thief, a liar, a heroin addict. I hate him. He stole our money, left the basement a shambles, reduced my wife to tears at the waste of money and time. I hate that he held my children, that he shook hands with my wife, that he ever set foot in my home. But if I believe that the gaunt ragged man who died between thieves on the Hill of Skulls was reborn, I have to look for Him in Walter. This is very difficult for me. But as long as love wriggles out of hate there is faith.

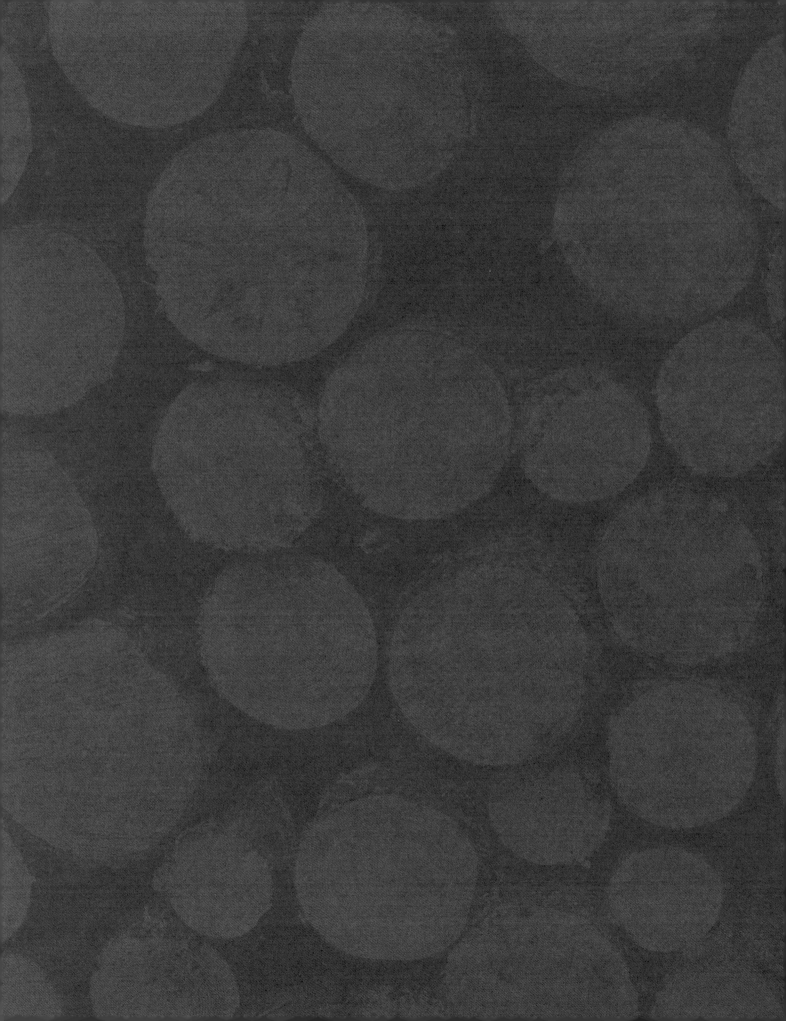

OF
WIND
AND
CEDAR

An Eye Opening

For many years I spent my weekends wandering along the shore of the Atlantic Ocean. I neither fished nor swam, and rarely did I venture out in my tiny red boat. Mostly I just shuffled along, watching the thousand creatures of the continent's edge: hawks, ducks, crabs, mussels, cormorants, sandpipers. On remote beaches I saw red foxes and blue herons; on urban beaches I saw water rats, brawling mobs of starlings, gangs of dusty pigeons.

Then I moved west. Now I walk by the Pacific Ocean and watch sea lions and grey whales, pelicans and eagles, seals and sea otters. Sometimes I wander among the soft coastal hills along the shore, hills that rise and swing like waves. Shorn of their ancient hemlock and cedar long ago, these hills have sprouted crewcuts of blackberry, alder, spruce, scrub oak. They are veined by old fire roads, abandoned logging roads, deer trails through impenetrable salal thickets.

Once I spent an entire summer day in those hills. For an hour I sat on a hillside watching wrens edit insects from the brush. For two hours I happily counted hummingbirds, and contemplated their frantic lives, and jumped when one materialized an inch from my considerable nose. It was a male, in full mating regalia, and he hung before me like a painting. I believe we were astonished by each other. I remember his furious pulse, his technicolor ruff, the boldness in his infinitesimal eye. His eye was the size of a pencil point. He was the size of a finger.

The look in his eye has stayed with me. He was alert, aware, absorbed, *alive*. Probably now he is dead; hummingbirds live fast and die young. What happened to the look in his eye? Did he glare at his Creator like he glared at me?

I stayed on that hillside all day. Near sunset I noticed a huge hawk circling over my head. He surfed lazily for a while and then wheeled and slid behind a hill. As he flared against the sun I noticed a notch sawn in his west wing. A flaw, a hole, a ragged badge of battle, it was only a space between feathers; but to me it suddenly seemed the first letter of a new alphabet, the opening of an idea, the eye of a creature too vast to name.

Meeting Marten

I should say right off that I have never actually met the fellow in the flesh, and that our interest has hardly been mutual, although it has persisted, in my case, for more than 30 years, ever since I pored over paintings of him in *Wild Mammals of North America* when I was ten years old and sprawled happily on a warm rug, riveted, for no reason I could tell then or now, by the family *Mustelidae*, the mammal family that begins small and ferocious with weasels and rises in heft and irascibility through mink, otter, skunk, marten, fisher, and badger to the wolverine, a creature so clever, powerful, and relentless in battle that even grizzly bears and cougars cede kills to it. The wolverine is legendary among woodsfolk for its eerie intelligence and terrific violence, but it is the much smaller pine marten that has fascinated me more over the years, and it is of this lithe arboreal creature, prince of the North American forest canopy, that I wish to speak.

Why would a man meditate for so long on a creature he has never seen and very probably will never see? I grow less lithe myself by the year, and busier with matters in towns and cities, and the chances of me wandering into the deep woods where martens gobble squirrels are near nil, for many good reasons. Yet I read books and articles about martens, and population studies, and field reports, and esoteric discussions of their reproductive capacities and litter sizes, and data of diet and habitat and physiology, and surveys of size (about two pounds, on average), and accounts of the marten's prehistoric ancestors, as big as dogs. I will never write books about martens, or make a living from the study of their lives, and I certainly could spend the time I give to martens in so many other nutritious ways, personal and professional. So why three decades of fascination with this creature of the deep boreal woods?

Perhaps *because* I will never see a marten, and so the creature is a metaphor for all that is wonderful beyond my ken. Perhaps because he is, like me, a furred appendaged warm-blooded North American carnivore who finds sustenance of various sorts in the forest. Perhaps because the natural histories of other creatures add substance and joy to our own lives, be those creatures avian, human, mammalian, piscine, or reptilian. We are irresistibly drawn to the tales of others because we need stories as much as food, because we eat stories, because too those stories are so often (at least) entertaining chronicles of hilarious misadventure or (at best) tales of immense wisdom and light.

So I read about the pine marten, and think with affection of him flying along the latticed branches of firs and cedars, a fist of grace and energy in the wet woods, wreaking havoc and despair among the order Rodentia, and I feel blessed by his story, by the knowledge that he is there in his joy as I am here in mine. To him my thanks; to the Mystery who carved him over so very many years, awe.

Pitter and Drench

Question from prospective student's mother, asked of me as we stand by the chapel on the most beautiful crisp sunlit October day you ever saw in your life: Does it rain here?

Does it *rain* here? Is the pope Jesuit? Is the ocean salty? Do swallows return in the spring? Are there still trees bigger than your house in the remote ravines of the dense moist forests of Cascadia? How do you think those trees got to be so epic? Did you know that those huge trees can drink water right out of the *air*? Do you think that a tree could get its water from the air without there being a lot of water in the air?

Does it *rain* here? Come back on All Souls Day, when the Rains begin with an indescribable gentle firm authority, so that you know, even before you are fully awake, that this is the Day, this is the beginning of the Wet, for the rain is thorough and relentless and inarguable, and this is not a shower, or a scatter, or a passing cloudburst, or a storm, but the opening bars of a very long song, the first chapter of a book that will take the next three seasons to read, the first minutes of a very long game, during which you will huddle under an umbrella, and thrash in the closet for your raincoat, and rub mink oil into your shoes yet again, and put that ratty old towel on the porch, so that when the dog wants to come in, some poor child has to kneel and wipe his muddy paws so he does not trot runes upon the floor I just this *minute* finished sweeping.

Does it *rain* here? Look about you, woman. Gaze long and lovingly on the lushness of the grass, and the vault of the trees, and the tangled insistence of the bushes, and the startling prevalence of moss, and the little swale near the chapel that is always moist no matter how hot and dry the weather, and tell me if you think that perhaps yes, a drop doth fall here and there, and then another, and then a thousand and million and uncountable zillions from November right through June, so that summer here is accounted from July through October, after which the Rains begin, and neither they do not cease, day after day after day of mist and rain and fog and drizzle and pitter and drench! Gaze about you piercingly at the endless ranks and shades of green across the river, and tell me if you think the long thicketed flank of the Tualatin Mountains is perhaps the product of uncountable years of the steadiest rain you could ever imagine! Gaze down upon the broad muscle of the river, and consider whence came all that water, which does not cease though the sun be bright, and almost doubles its serpentine girth in spring, when months of rain and weeks of snowmelt send a rush and roar of immense proportions to the sea, the Water from which all things came, including, in a sense, us!

Does it *rain* here? Madame, it does. But rather than groan and moan about it, let us consider it an extraordinary gift from the One: falling free and fresh from the sky every blessed day here on The Bluff is clean water, untouched and untrammeled by the greedy hand of man; and so let us step inside the chapel, and thank that which once called itself *I Am Who Am*, Who giveth us profligately the sweet and savory rain; and so amen.

What the River Thinks

voles. Water striders
mosquitos mosquito-hawks.
Dock and dewberry. Moths and
mergansers. Huckleberry and snowberry.
Hawks and osprey. Water wheels and beaver dams.
Deer and lupine. Red currant. Trees and logs and trunks and
branches and bark and duff. I eat everything. Elderberry and
evening primrose. Bulrush and burdock. I know them all. They
yearn for me. Caddis fly and coralroot. I do not begin nor do
I cease. Foamflower fleeceflower fireweed. I always am always
will be. Lily and lotus. Swell and surge and ripple and roar and
roil and boil. I go to the Mother. Madrone and mistmaiden. The
Mother takes me in. Nettle and ninebark. Pelt and peppergrass.
She waits for me. Pine-sap and poppy. I bring her all small
waters. Raspberry and rockcress. I draw them I lure them I
accept them. Salal and satin-flower. She is all waters. Tansy and
trillium. She drinks me. Velvetgrass and vernalgrass. I begin as
a sheen on leaves high in the hills, a wet idea, a motion, a
dream, a rune, and then I am a ripple, and I gather small waters
to me, the little wet children, the rills of the hills, and we are
me and run to Her muscling through wood and stone cutting
through everything singing and shouting roiling and rippling
and there She is waiting and whispering her salty arms always
opening always open always o.

Salmon and steelhead and cutthroat trout. Fir needles. Salmonberries dropping suddenly and being snapped up by trout
who think them orange insects. Alder and spruce roots drinking
me always their eager thin little rude roots poking at me. Rocks
and pebbles and grains of stone and splinters of stone and huge
stones and slabs and beaver and mink and crawdads and feces
from the effluent treatment plant upriver. Rain and mist and fog
and gale and drizzle and howl and owl. Asters and arrow-grass.
Finger creeks feeder creeks streams ditches seeps and springs.
Row-boats and rafts. Canoes and chicory. Men and women and
children. Dead and alive. Willows and beer bottles and blackberry and ducklings and wood sorrel and rubber boots and
foxglove and buttercup and rushes and slugs and snails and
velvetgrass and wild cucumber and orbweaver spiders. Bane-
berry and beargrass. Thrush and hemlock and coffee grounds.
Thimbleberry and heron. Smelt and moss and water ouzels
and bears and bear scat. Elk drinking me cougar drinking me.
Ground-cedar and ground-ivy and ground-pine and groundsel.
Sometimes a lost loon. Cinquefoil and eelgrass. Vultures and

PERHAPS...

In Otter Words

One day I
am sitting at my old
desk reading young essays,
these are essays sent to me by
holy children of various sizes, and
I can feel the joy sloshing and rising
in me as their words pour in, and finally
I get topped off by the phrase *in otter words*,
a child has scrawled this in the brightest green
ink you ever saw, *in otter words, the holy parts
are circled*, she writes, and I think maybe my head
is going to fly off, and what remains of my shaggy
brain sprints away giggling and mooing with pleasure.
You know how it's said that human beings are the only
creatures who can contemplate two ideas at once? It's
even better than that — we can entertain *lots* of joyous
ideas at once, it turns out. Such as, o my god, *otter
words,* that's enough right there for hours of happy
speculation, am I right? I mean, what *are* the otter
words for trout and rain and minnows and ice and
fur that has been warmed by the sun to just the
right sheen and shimmer? I bet there *are* otter
words for that, and for clumsy fishermen,
and for looming osprey, and for velvet
mud of exactly the right consistency
for sliding in, and for dying
chinook salmon like ancient
riddled kings, and
brilliant red drift
boats, and

cocky young mergansers,
and huge brooding herons, and falcons
falling like fists, and the basso murmur of
mossy boulders grumbling at the bottom of the river, and
the tinny querulous voices of crawdads, and the speed-freak
chitter of chickadees, and the fat feet of tiny kids, and the little
pebbly houses that caddisflies live in, and the salmonflies like tiny
orange helicopters. And *the holy parts!* which are *circled*, we knew that was
true, the holy parts *are* underlined and illuminated and highlighted, aren't
they, and circled with a huge honking blessed magic marker as big as a beaver,
isn't that so? Sometimes I feel like the eyes in my heart sludge closed quietly without
me paying much attention, and I muddle and mutter along thinking I am savoring
and celebrating, and then *wham* a kid, it's always a kid, says something so piercing and
wild and funny and unusual that *wham* my heart eyes fly open again like doors flung
open by, say, an otter, and *wham,* I am completely and utterly overwhelmed and thrilled
by the shocking brilliant uniforms that falcons wear, and rendered speechless by the
roiling summer seas of my wife's eyes, and I get the shivering willies hearing my dad's gentle
snortling laugh on the phone, and my *god* have you ever seen a blue jay up close and personal,
what a cheerful arrogant criminal it is, all brass and swagger, isn't that so? And most of all, best
of all, better than every other joy and thrill, even the very best beer, which is a *very* excellent
thing, are kids. Sure, they learn to lie, and sure, they are just not as into dental hygiene as you
wish they were, and my *god* they skin their knees nine times a day, and do things like smear
peanut butter on their abraded knees just to see what it feels like, and shake flour on the dog!
so that when he shakes off the flour at one million shimmers per minute there will be a flour
cloud in the kitchen the size of Utah!, isn't that *cool* dad?, but more than anything else
in the world it is kids who make us see that the holy parts are circled. You know and I
know this is true. We forget. I think maybe we should write it down somewhere, like
in magic marker on the wall by the stove, or in steamy words on the bathroom
mirror, so we will see it every day, and remember it, and be refreshed to the
bottom of our bony bottoms. If necessary use otter words.

Under Western Waters

Tir na nOg, the Country of the Young, my Irish forebears called it, and it was to the west always, and many said it was a country under the western waters. A blessed land it was, "for age and death have not found it, neither tears nor loud laughter have gone near it," noted William Butler Yeats, who was absorbed by legends of it as the favorite haunt of the *doaine sidhe*, the fairies, whom you would address as *doaine maithe*, the good people, as they are easily offended, being perhaps the former heroes of ancient Ireland, *Tuatha De Danan*, now reduced and dwindled in the imagination, and thus physically reduced to creatures only a few hands high, and found only in remote places, like dells and groves and dingles and quiet creeks, and in the Country of the Young, which would sometimes appear shimmering on the western sea to those who watched from the cliffs of Cork and Kerry, Clare and Galway, Mayo and Sligo and Donegal.

Although some said too that Tir na nOg could be found under holy lakes, such visions of it always accompanied by the sound of bells, and others said it could be reached only on the back of a white horse, as did the poet Oisin, who dwelt there three hundred years, returning finally for love of his friends, but upon dismounting from his horse, suddenly aged those years, and was instantly bowed by time and bearded greatly; yet before his death he spoke of the Country of the Young to Saint Patrick, who told of it ever after.

When *An Gorta Mor* came to Ireland, the great famine, and men and women and children thin as laths fled the horror, they mostly fled into the west, away from the imperial English who had starved them, away from the death eating their nation, away over the western waters, toward the country of the living. In America their children and children's children drove west too, always west, the land of promise and chance, where Meriwether Lewis and William Clark found a new creature every single day of their odyssey. And many years later a thread of clan Dubhghaill, the dark strangers, as we were called in the mountains of County Wicklow by the waters of the Irish Sea, came to rest here against the Pacific Ocean, and now my small children leave out milk and apples for the *sheagh sidhe*, the fairy host, and see the flickering lights of the good people amid firs and fern, and find, in summer, circles of flattened grass where the fairies have been at play.

I have seen my children standing on the beach here in the West, staring fixedly at the sea, for no reason they can easily name; and while there are those who say we are as riveted unaccountably by great waters as we are by fire and stars, also vast and fluid creatures, I say that they are looking for Tir na nOg, the land of eternal grace, where neither death nor tears will afflict them, where we will love each other forever, where *geabhaedh tu an sonas aer pighin*, we will find happiness as common as pennies.

Original Skin

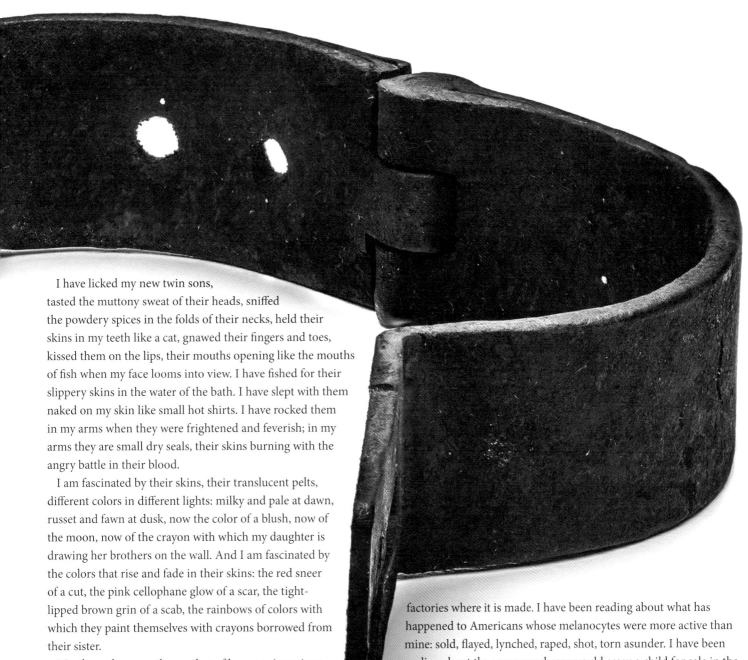

I have licked my new twin sons, tasted the muttony sweat of their heads, sniffed the powdery spices in the folds of their necks, held their skins in my teeth like a cat, gnawed their fingers and toes, kissed them on the lips, their mouths opening like the mouths of fish when my face looms into view. I have fished for their slippery skins in the water of the bath. I have slept with them naked on my skin like small hot shirts. I have rocked them in my arms when they were frightened and feverish; in my arms they are small dry seals, their skins burning with the angry battle in their blood.

I am fascinated by their skins, their translucent pelts, different colors in different lights: milky and pale at dawn, russet and fawn at dusk, now the color of a blush, now of the moon, now of the crayon with which my daughter is drawing her brothers on the wall. And I am fascinated by the colors that rise and fade in their skins: the red sneer of a cut, the pink cellophane glow of a scar, the tight-lipped brown grin of a scab, the rainbows of colors with which they paint themselves with crayons borrowed from their sister.

Mostly my boys are the gentlest of browns. At various times in various moods they are chamois, chestnut, cinnamon, ochre, sepia, taupe, umber, walnut, the color of cougars, the color of old bones, the color of dust and dusk. Every time I touch them they are a new color in my hands, my hands cracked and leathery old saddles laid on the glistening gold coats of my colts.

I have been reading about skin: its layers, its glands, its magical sensory and insulatory properties. I have been reading about tyrosine, from which skin pigment is made, and tyrosinase, the enzyme that makes it, and melanocytes, the infinitesimal

factories where it is made. I have been reading about what has happened to Americans whose melanocytes were more active than mine: sold, flayed, lynched, raped, shot, torn asunder. I have been reading about the way a purchaser would assay a child for sale in the slave markets of this nation, by running his hand over the child's skin, feeling for irregularities, feeling for weaknesses, feeling for an inferior product. I have been reading about a slave auction in Carolina in the last century, at which "two Nigro boys, twins, two Year old," were sold to different masters, and I have been hearing the jagged roars of their dark father in his own dark chains, his utter anguish and rage and horror, and I have been hearing the awful screams of his boys as they are carried away from each other and from him, their choking sobs haunting him the rest of his broken life, haunting me this sweet coppery summer morning, haunting us all.

Mr. Lincoln

He gave his life for the extraordinary American idea.
Do not let that idea die.

He oversaw a savage war in which many hundreds of thousands of American boys and men died and hundreds of battles were fought on American soil and in American waters. Many thousands of boys and men from other countries died in the horrors also. Many thousands of girls and women were injured and raped and terrorized and hammered and haunted the rest of their days. He was often a melancholic man riven by sadness. He was so deeply private and guarded about his deepest feelings that even the people who knew him best did not know the bottomless depths of his faith in a Coherent Mercy. According to one friend he was utterly hapless at reading faces and motivations in others, though he was possessed of the deepest and most extraordinary empathy. Two of his three sons died as boys and he never recovered from such grievous losses of those he loved. He was sometimes so blunt and artless that people thought he was playing games upon their credulity. He loved lewd and vulgar and inane and rude jokes and laughed uproariously at them no matter what the company or the setting. He was apparently incapable of lying or disseminating or bending the truth. He said himself that he was all his life a fatalist, and believed that the Lord would make of him such a tool as was necessary for the times at hand. He was a poor manager of money and among the least ambitious of men as regards the getting and keeping of same, which is why he was always in debt or teetering on its precipice. He was by every account a homely man, with a bristling tangle of hair, and a lanky face like a cliff of riven granite, and hands like the gnarled branches of an old tree. He was so cautious and meticulous and patient in his thinking that some people meeting him for the first time thought him simple.

He was not simple in the least. *He was the only man I ever knew the foundation of whose spirit was love*, wrote a friend. He liked to carry his son on his shoulder and they walked everywhere hand in hand. He supervised and agonized over the war that murdered hundreds of thousands of people because he could not stand the idea of Americans not walking hand in hand toward the extraordinary country we could be, a country unlike any other that ever was, a country where all citizens are free to speak their hearts, and gather as they like, and worship whatever shape of holiness they perceive or imagine, and offer their love to whom they like. He would not allow his beloved country to fly apart because of greed and lies, and for that he was murdered by a man whose greatest wish was to tear America in half.

It is a foul and evil lie of the mind and the heart and the mouth and the soul to account someone less because of his or her color or religion or gender or preference in lovers. That is a squirming lie, no matter how often, and at what volume, it is repeated. It is an ancient lie and it has cursed our species for a million years and God willing it will be quelled and squelched and forgotten in the years to come. It will be squelched not by laws and regulations, not by political or religious or judicial powers, but by shivers of dawning light in the hearts of men and women and children in this country who begin to dimly understand that Abraham Lincoln was the greatest of Americans not because he won a war, not because he gave his blood and his life for justice and freedom, but because the foundation of his spirit was love, *and he acted that way.* He was a devout man who called no one religion his home. As every religion claims to be an agent of holiness, so every political party claims to be the avatar of the best and deepest aspects of the American character and idea; but if that were so, we would begrudgingly hold hands, and reluctantly agree that we are equal each to each, and must treat each other with honesty and humility; that we will, by the grace of the profligate gifts granted us as Americans, stand for and speak for and defend and protect freedom anywhere and everywhere it is savaged; that we will continue to, as we have for centuries, open our golden door for the tired and the poor, the huddled masses, the wretched of the world, and here let them breathe free; and that differences in color and gender and religion and preference in love matter not at all when it comes to treating each other with respect and reverence. Those who fan and foment differences murder the revolutionary American idea, and ought to cower and gibber in shame in the vast shadow cast by Mr. Abraham Lincoln, Republican of Kentucky, who gave his life for that idea.

Their Irrepressible

Whenever I find myself growing grim about the mouth; whenever it is a moist gray November in my soul; whenever I find myself slathered by lies and poseurs, afflicted by devious performance art at every turn, and grimly expecting the worst of every situation and every person I meet; whenever I find myself expecting to be cut off in traffic, to be shortchanged at the store, to hear an ominous clank in the transmission, to catch a cold, to be ludicrously overbilled by the insurance company, to find the library closed early, to endure computer malfunction, to find the wine sour, to lose my keys, to hear of sudden surgery in the tribe, to discover a city of slugs in the cellar, and to find a dead owlet under the cracked front picture window, then I account it high time to get to a kindergarten as fast as I can, and sit myself down in a tiny chair, looking not unlike a large hairy bespectacled bookish giant, and inquire of the lives and dreams and feats of the small populace, and listen with the most assiduous and ferocious attention, for I find that as few as twenty minutes with people no taller than your belt buckle is enormously refreshing, and gloriously educational, and wonderfully startling, and endlessly hilarious, and very much like drinking a tremendous

glass of crystalline water when you have been desperately thirsty for a long time, and in something of a personal desert.

They will tell you of the animals with whom they speak cheerfully and at length every day, and explain carefully what the animals say in return, speaking sometimes with their noses and their feet and their fingers. They will tell you of their dreams in which they are swifter than falcons and bigger than bears. They will tell you of their futures when they are absolutely going to be dancers and pilots and firefighters. They will tell you of the strange wild mysterious people in their lives, some of them visible and some not, as yet. They will talk knowledgeably of angels and spirits and voices that come out of the ground if you dig a deep enough hole. They will speak other languages than ones you know or they know. They will sing with or without the slightest provocation or solicitation. They love to explain things by drawing them, and colors for them have flavors and characters and tonal intimations and strict rules and regulations; depending on the artist, you can use green for buffalo, but you cannot use blue for cougars, because cougars are *afraid of blue*, everyone knows that.

Innocence

If you draw them out and give them time and afford them the clear sense that you are not judging or assessing or measuring them in any way, they will stretch out and tell you tales of adventure and derring-do that would make filmmakers and novelists drool. They hold hands and kiss each other without the slightest self-consciousness or social awareness. They suddenly break off conversations to do headstands because when a headstand needs to be done it should be done without delay. They are inordinately proud of their socks and show you their socks at every opportunity, and you never saw such a wild welter of bright animated colorfully patterned socks in your life as those in kindergartens: It is Sock Paradise. They use the word cubby all the time, which is a pleasant rotund word that we should use more often. When they are released into the schoolyard or the playground they sprint out into the welcoming embrace of the wild green world with all their might, with their arms flung open and their mouths open and their shoes untied, and when I see this from my tiny chair, when I see them fling themselves howling and thrilling into the delicious world that arose miraculously from the emptiness of the vast unknowable universe, I weep at their joy, and at some other thing I do not understand — their irrepressible innocence, my battered innocence, our assaulted endangered innocence, their clean fresh unconscious grace, the fraught teetering of our species; and then I arise, and thank the teacher for allowing me to visit, and drive home, restored.

STORY
CATCHER

Soul Spans

Here are some bridge stories. Once an old man to whom I had not spoken for months although we were neighbors called me up in the middle of the night to help him pull in his beach stairs. Our houses were on the edge of the ocean and the ocean was furious. Out I went to meet him, in the slicing wind, and we pulled up his stairs, and I tore my hands, and shook his hand, and did not help him limp back to his house, because he was a proud and good man, as I learned later, after we met on the bridge he had made with his words.

Once I hammered a man with my fists. This was on a muddy field long ago. We punched each other until he bled and I cried with rage and exhaustion and we were pulled apart by other men. I saw him the next day in the street. We hated each other and then he smiled. His smile was a bridge that shamed me.

Recently a friend of mine died. He was 23. I wrote a letter to his mother about his hands, which were enormous and deft. She wrote back: a small gray card, a few quiet words, her name. The card was a bridge between despair and peace.

Recently my wife was very sick. She lay in her hospital bed like a rag. She was in a pale country far from me. I kissed her with a joke in my mouth, desperate for her smile. She smiled. The leap of her lips was a bridge between lovers.

Once, long ago, when I was a small boy, I wrote a letter to my mother and left it under her plate on Mother's Day. It was a letter from Hell, refusing her admission. My father sent this letter to a small magazine, which published it and sent me a check for $10. I still have that check. It is the bridge by which I became a writer.

This morning I ate breakfast with my daughter. She is an angel with an attitude, two years old. Suddenly she turned and kissed me on the nose. Her kiss was made of cinnamon and milk and it was a bridge to my hoary heart.

We are bound, you and I, by ink and paper and a university high above a river. I sit here and tell you about myself; back come your stories, sad and merry and honest. It is a curious conversation, poignant and surprising. I am moved by it. It is a gift and a lesson. It is a bridge.

Smoke

Here's a story. A man steers a landing craft onto a beach in the Philippines in 1944. He is rescuing as many soldiers as he can get off the beach. He is a corporal. The soldiers have been trapped on the beach under fire all day and all night for more than a month. They are the last ragged bloody shred of a much larger troop of soldiers. All the other soldiers who were on the beach are dead.

Soldiers from the other side of the war fire bullets and missile shells at the corporal as fast as they can get the bullets and shells out of their guns. The bullets and shells scream and shriek over the corporal's head.

The corporal frantically loads 28 soldiers into his boat and then guns it off the beach as fast as he can go.

When the boat is safely out to sea he cuts the engines and goes to each man and kneels down and looks into his eyes.

Their eyes are remote and stunned and empty. They are pretty much zombies, those guys, he says. The corporal offers them coffee but none of them want coffee.

He offers them food but none of them want food.

But then he walks around the boat offering each man a cigarette, and they *do* want cigarettes, so he goes around his crowded boat, one man at a time, and lights a smoke, and reaches down gently, and tips the stunned soldier's helmet up, and places the cigarette in the man's lips; and every time he does this, every time he reaches down gently and tips a helmet and places his offering in the lips of a hollow hopeless boy, he feels a wrench in his heart.

Many years later he tells me this story and he says, you know, cigarettes killed my dad, and I hated em all my life, from when I was a boy right up into now, and I roared at my children when they tried em, like kids do you know, and my wife and I had six kids, so that's a lot of roaring. But you know, that day on the beach, I can't explain it, if ever there was a day when they weren't coffin nails, if ever there was a day when they were holy things, when giving a man a smoke was some kind of prayer or something, a kind of communion or something, well, I tell you, that was the day.

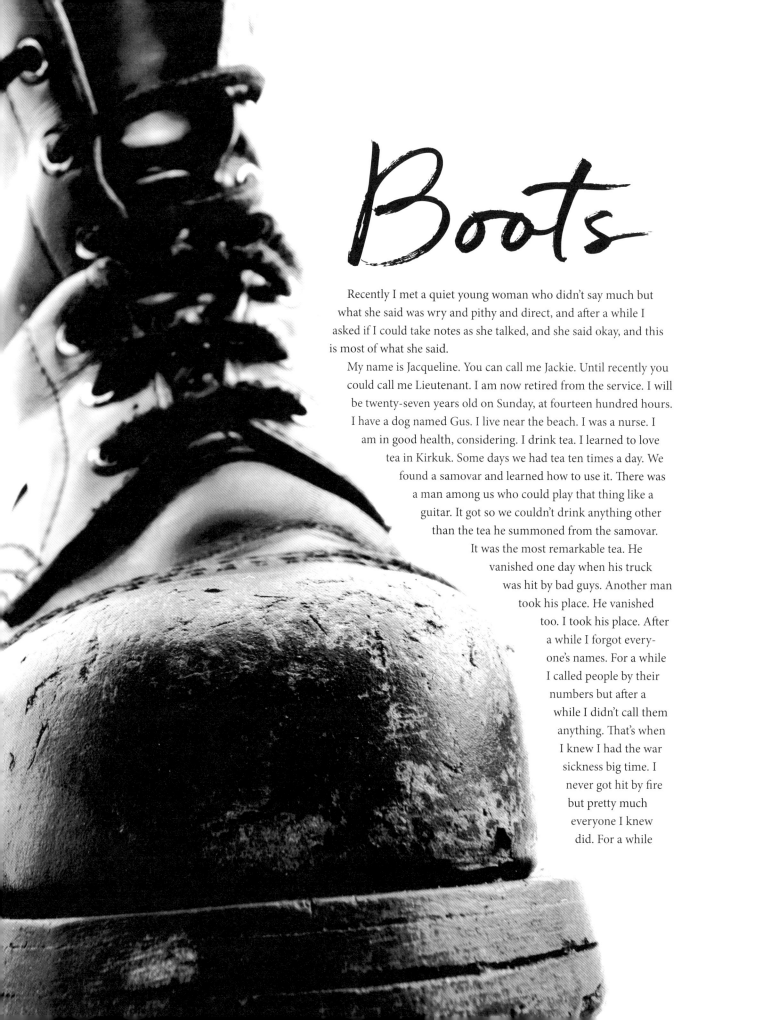

Boots

Recently I met a quiet young woman who didn't say much but what she said was wry and pithy and direct, and after a while I asked if I could take notes as she talked, and she said okay, and this is most of what she said.

My name is Jacqueline. You can call me Jackie. Until recently you could call me Lieutenant. I am now retired from the service. I will be twenty-seven years old on Sunday, at fourteen hundred hours. I have a dog named Gus. I live near the beach. I was a nurse. I am in good health, considering. I drink tea. I learned to love tea in Kirkuk. Some days we had tea ten times a day. We found a samovar and learned how to use it. There was a man among us who could play that thing like a guitar. It got so we couldn't drink anything other than the tea he summoned from the samovar. It was the most remarkable tea. He vanished one day when his truck was hit by bad guys. Another man took his place. He vanished too. I took his place. After a while I forgot everyone's names. For a while I called people by their numbers but after a while I didn't call them anything. That's when I knew I had the war sickness big time. I never got hit by fire but pretty much everyone I knew did. For a while

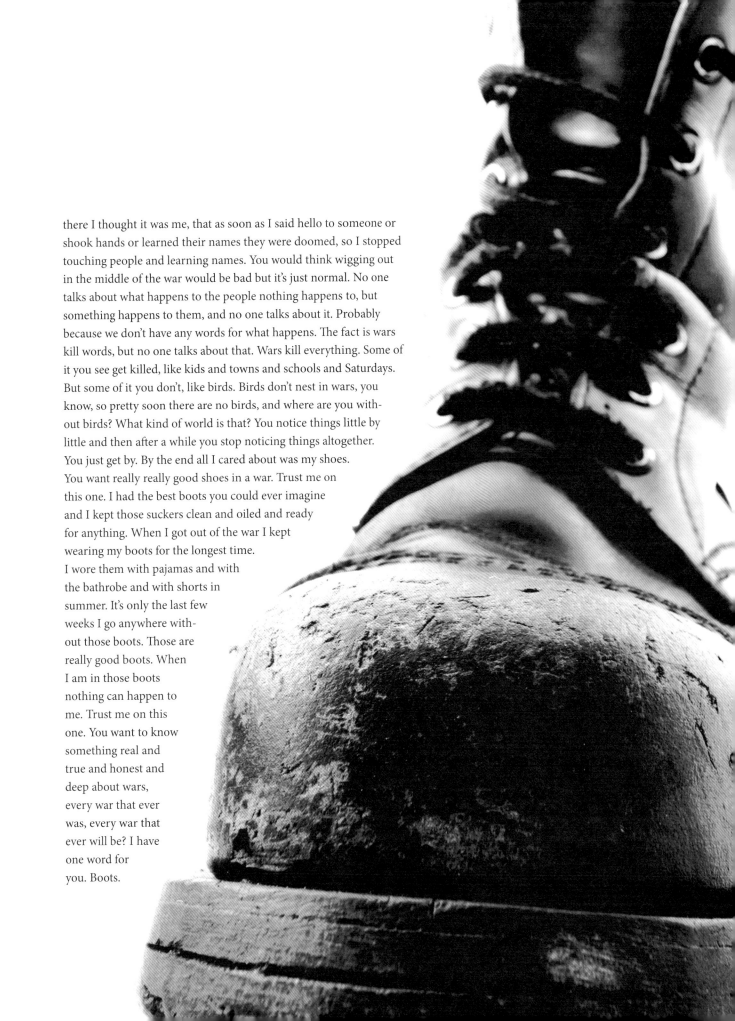

there I thought it was me, that as soon as I said hello to someone or shook hands or learned their names they were doomed, so I stopped touching people and learning names. You would think wigging out in the middle of the war would be bad but it's just normal. No one talks about what happens to the people nothing happens to, but something happens to them, and no one talks about it. Probably because we don't have any words for what happens. The fact is wars kill words, but no one talks about that. Wars kill everything. Some of it you see get killed, like kids and towns and schools and Saturdays. But some of it you don't, like birds. Birds don't nest in wars, you know, so pretty soon there are no birds, and where are you without birds? What kind of world is that? You notice things little by little and then after a while you stop noticing things altogether. You just get by. By the end all I cared about was my shoes. You want really really good shoes in a war. Trust me on this one. I had the best boots you could ever imagine and I kept those suckers clean and oiled and ready for anything. When I got out of the war I kept wearing my boots for the longest time. I wore them with pajamas and with the bathrobe and with shorts in summer. It's only the last few weeks I go anywhere without those boots. Those are really good boots. When I am in those boots nothing can happen to me. Trust me on this one. You want to know something real and true and honest and deep about wars, every war that ever was, every war that ever will be? I have one word for you. Boots.

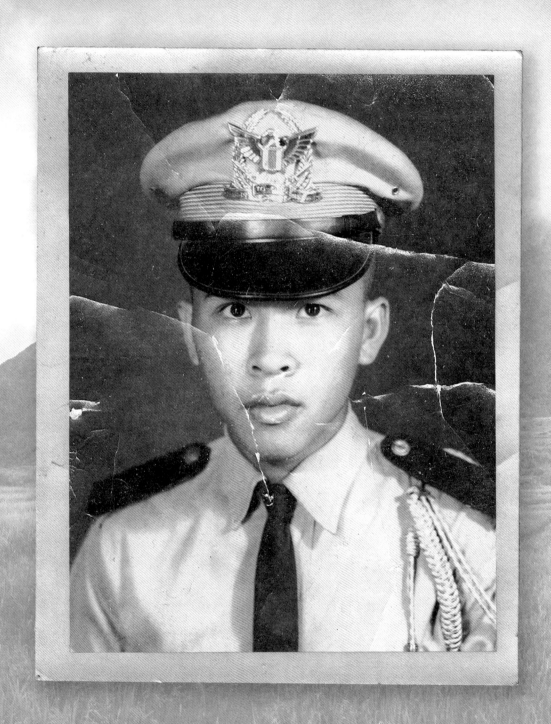

No

No Van Vo is a brief man with one eye and one foot. He is a mechanic at the University. He can fix anything and has done so here for six years. He was born in Vietnam. When he was eighteen years old he sat for the national college exam there. Students who passed the exam went on to university and students who failed went into the army. He failed the exam and went into the army. His army was at war. One day he stepped on a land mine and lost his left foot and his left eye and most of his right eye. Then the other army overran his army and that was the end of the war.

Former sergeants in the wrong army were not popular with the new government, and there wasn't much work in the new Vietnam for blind one-legged men, of which there were thousands after thirty years of war, and No didn't want to lean on the largesse of his family, so he applied for emigration, which was denied, and his sister tried to buy him a spot on a clandestine boat, but her money was stolen.

So I concluded to escape, he says.

I decided to cross the border to Cambodia, he says. My father and I cried. I sold all my clothes. All I had left was shorts and a shirt and cigarettes and my plastic foot. I took a riverboat to the border. Some guys showed me where to go. We waited for dusk. They took off running fast through the fields and I followed them. I carried my crutch on my shoulder and ran as fast as I could. We got across the border into Cambodia. The Khmer Rouge were in charge there. I went west, toward Thailand. I didn't have any money. A boy in a village was supposed to help me go through the forest into Thailand but he left me in the forest. I got caught by soldiers and sent back to the village.

Then that village was attacked by other soldiers. We lay on the floor as bullets and mortar shells fell all around. We could hear the soldiers shouting. We were on the floor for a day and a night. Worries came up through my mind.

To escape into Thailand you needed about a hundred dollars. So a woman said she would take me through the forest and across the border in a wagon. The forest was filled with robbers and soldiers. At the border the soldiers put me in jail. I was there for two weeks. I prayed for good luck. There was only rice soup and salt to eat. The women in that prison were raped every night. Then one day the head of the prison saw me limping and falling in the mud. When he found out I was blind and crippled he told his soldiers to get rid of me because I couldn't do any work for them.

Instead of killing me they gave me to the Red Cross and the Red Cross put me in a refugee camp on the border. I was there for one year. One day all the handicapped people in camp were moved to another place and a week later some soldiers attacked the first camp and burned it to the ground and killed everyone they could find.

Because I had been in our army when your army and our army were fighting on the same side in the war I could come to your country, which I did. Some people helped me get a cornea transplant. When I opened my eye after the operation everything was very bright. I was *very* happy to see again. I studied to be a mechanic. I met my wife here and we have two boys now. They are very intelligent boys.

I went back to Vietnam two years ago but no one recognized me. I don't blame them. It was a very long time ago that I was there. A very long time ago.

The Cedar People

The people who used to live in Portland had russet skin. They lived here for four thousand years. No one knows what they called themselves. We call them Chinook, which may have meant *don't point your finger at me* in their language. Many of them had red hair. They built enormous houses of cedar with ceilings twenty feet high. In the soft rain they wore waterproof hats and robes of woven cedar. They used cedar for diapers, canoes, masks, drums,

arrows,
paddles,
cradles, harpoons,
rakes, weirs, looms, nets,
rattles, rope, bowls, horns, whistles,
blankets, and baskets, among other things.
In winter they wore vests made of otter and bear.
In summer they painted themselves purple and invented sunbathing. They flattened the foreheads of their children and considered the shaped head a sign of aristocracy and enslaved their roundheaded neighbors where possible. In battle, a rare event, they wore armor made of dried elk leather. They liked to drink sea lion oil, a delicacy. They ate salmonberries, thimbleberries, gooseberries, bearberries, shotberries. When one of their children died her toys and dishes were left outside to bleach and fade, their colors leaching away at the same rate as her parents' pain. The way to win their favorite game was to remain straightfaced as a circle of people told jokes. The way to become respected among them was to give away the most things. In their world names were momentous and had to be earned by deeds or dreams. Sometimes old people would hand over their tired names to their children and take fresh names with which to die. They knew hundreds of stories and could tell them for many hours. A strong man during the height of the salmon run could catch eight tons of fish in a day. They ate salmon broiled, baked, poached, roasted, smoked, salted, and hammered into sheets as thin and dry as pink paper. By some accounts the women sang all day long. When they died they were placed in canoes that were hoisted into the sky river on poles. They spoke two languages, their own and a trading tongue spoken among Indian peoples wherever there was serious winter rain. A few words of that language are still alive: *tyee, skookum, tillicum, potlatch.*

A great sickness came to them in the summer of 1830 and they died, whole families and villages and clans dead in weeks. The sickness may have been malaria. No one knows. A few people survived but they were lonely and disheartened and after the sickness they built only small houses with low ceilings. After a while they died too and soon there were no more cedar people. Yet the land is soaked with their voices and stories, and so here they are still, with their red hair and berry-stained skins, trying not to laugh, giving everything away.

FOREVER
FRIENDS

# Ed

Summer reminds me, God knows why, of my friend Ed, who is a whole species of man unto himself, the only one of his kind, the very archetype and all possible subsequent permutations of Edness in his own singular person. He is sensible, brilliant, unusually accomplished — he's a neurosurgeon of great skill, a self-taught beekeeper, a sailor who has survived gales from hell, a husband, a father — yet he is also liable to being riveted suddenly and irretrievably by reef topography, canine physiology, or the history of collegiate eating clubs, and he can be utterly absorbed beyond recall at any hour, in any social situation, whether or not he is supposed to roast the roast or toast the toast.

This capacity for ferocious concentration is perhaps what makes him such a deft man with a scalpel, but it also drives his family and friends to distraction or delight, depending on the Eddish event. I think, for example, of the night he was supposed to be making coffee for many guests but became entranced by a clockmaker's explanation of the innards of ancient timepieces; or the summer he decided that lawns were best mowed at dawn; or his long and ultimately fruitless devotion to a Chevrolet Impala, an affair which ended finally in acrimonious divorce; or the year he became enamored of curry and single-handedly kept the economy of India humming; or the way in which he cheerfully shaved his head when his wife lost her locks to cancer; or the way in which his casual apiary interest turned into a jillion jars of honey and enthusiastic entomological lectures; or the boundless pleasure with which he explains to a patient how he will make an incision here and here, and remove the top of the brain like a sardine can, and then go in and see what we can see, and nip and tuck a bit, and get everything shipshape, and then put everything back together in approximately the same order as before, and you'll be a new man by nightfall, God willing, although you'll have a new religion and you'll be left-handed.

The face of the patient to whom he delivers this talk is a pearl without price.

You have but to meet Ed and you are Edified and Educated; the man is a force of nature, true to himself in every particular, forged by Russian Jewish parents, blessed by marriage to a Catholic girl from Idaho who once exploded a pie in a state baking contest, and graced finally by two children, male and female, who only grin when asked to explain their father, and it is this grin that seems to me a wonderfully summery thing, a flash of love in a world of pain, a warm pause in a cold year.

Their father — that amiable man over there talking to his bees, and due at the hospital in an hour — is a tale never before told and never to be told again, which is, of course, your story, and mine, and a stunning miracle; and so, on a bright summer morning, this Editorial.

Rich Rich Rich Rich

Phone rings as I am washing the dishes for the 900,000th time. Daughter runs for the phone. Daughter is twelve years old and addicted to phone. Not me — I hate the phone.

I yell *Don't answer it!*

She answers it.

She brings me the phone. My arms are soap to the elbows. I prepare to snarl but I see her face and I dry my hands and take the phone.

It's my old friend Danno who always makes me laugh. Not this time. This time he is calling from the hospital where his daughter is dying. She got hit by a truck and broke everything you can break and she just received the last rites.

She's twenty-two years old. She just graduated from college. She just had a baby boy. The boy is two months old.

I remember when this boy's mama was two months old. She slept in the top drawer of a rickety bureau. Her folks had about seven cents when she was born. All these years later they don't have much more than seven cents but they had three more children after Julie and my friend Dan would say, grinning, *we are rich rich rich rich*, and he meant it, too, even though they were never a hint of rich, and his wife's been sick for years, and the black dog has chased through their clan, and one child once had a fever so virulent and savage that it sent the boy into a wheelchair for a while, and my friend has worked so hard and so long and at so many jobs at once to support his family that his hair went bone white before he was thirty, and a piece of his back broke once and he wept himself to sleep every night for a year, but all through his ocean of pain he has grinned and laughed and sang, and never have I met a man with such a heart, and I love him dearly, and I tell him that on the phone, and he says I love you too you mangy mule, and I chant the names of all his old girlfriends to make him laugh, which he does, I can hear him laughing in the hallway of the hospital far away, and then he says *I hafta go, pray for Jules*, and we hang up and I pray helplessly into the sink, into the bubbles and apple peels.

I pray for my friend and his family to be rich rich rich rich and not rich rich rich.

I pray down into the cups and forks, the crusts of pizza my children refuse to eat, which drives me nuts, but I say aloud to the soggy crusts *rich rich rich rich*, which makes me cry, and I wash off the crusts and dry them and carry them out to the grass for the crows to eat for some reason I don't understand that has everything to do with praying for Julie.

A Sporting Man

Within days of his arrival as a freshman in 1933 he was sweating and sprinting as one of the University's football players, and over the years I came to especially savor his football stories, all of them rife with humor and abounding with the mud and muscle and verve of the game he loved first and best, the game that bent his nose and mashed his fingers and filled his young heart with joy. Later he would box — badly and briefly, by his own amused account — but as his undergraduate years lengthened his interests widened, and by his junior year he was both president of his class and a *Beacon* reporter of grace and skill.

Forced by the Depression to leave school, forced to find work to help feed his family, he labored in the wheat fields of Oregon, and then in the woods and rivers of Idaho; and then came the war, during which the United States Army Air Corps put him to work in its intelligence corps in Italy and North Africa, his opponent across the line now a real enemy, cold and murderous. Like most

soldiers he did his task well while hating it, and he spoke of the war only to remember his companions in that dark work.

After the war he came back to The Bluff, finished his degree, and lent the University his myriad and cheerful talents as news director, *Alumni Bulletin* editor, career advisor, yearbook advisor, alumni secretary, and general jack of whatever trades needed jacking, until 1950, when again he left campus, this time for 28 years afield as a newspaperman and public relations man. Upon retiring from those creative professions he returned a third time to campus, as an editor, and in that capacity he

devoted 20 more years to the University he held close to his heart, until that heart finally failed him and he died, surrounded by his family, on the last day of summer.

He worked down the hall from me for seven years, in the same building where he was a student dreaming of girls and glory in the 1930s. His office was mere yards from the muddy field where he played football for the Pilots, from Howard Hall where he boxed in Monogram Club smokers, from the Clark Library that housed him for thousands of hours, from the blessed spot on campus where in 1949 he first spied a lovely young nursing professor named Gabrielle Huys, to whom he instantly paid court and with whom he soon shared marriage and then three sons.

In my four decades on this earth I never met a more generous man, nor one more patient with folly, nor one so brave under duress. He was what the University stands to be: intelligent, responsible, independent, kind, attentive, graceful, alert to divinity, liable to humor, profligate with love, true to his companions, averse to machination, possessed of a dignity born not of position or place but of character as sound as the great trees of his native land. This man was my dear friend Robert Boehmer '37, who graced the University with his affections and talents for many decades until his matriculation, on a bright summer afternoon, at another university, in which the curriculum is peace eternal and joy unending. May he rest in peace.

His Father

Well, here's a story I never told before, but it's been haunting me, so I think I have to tell it, because I'm pretty sure no one else will, and if a story doesn't get told, isn't that a door that never gets a chance to open, and isn't that a shame and a sin?

So then.

I was in college. This was in the middle of America thirty years ago. It was the last night I was ever in college. There was a huge roaring tumultuous party in our hall. It was a very old hall with ironwork everywhere and vaulted ceilings and all the students who were not graduating yet had gone home so our hall echoed with music and shouting and laughter and chaos and merriment. Of course almost every student who was about to graduate had family members arriving for the weekend, so a few sisters and brothers and even a dad or two joined the party, and everyone tried to chat up the new girls, and then people from other halls who heard the roar from our hall wandered over, and soon it was midnight and the party was throbbing and even the shyest people were dancing and giggling and shouting. It was a really great party.

At about one in the morning I noticed that the dad of a friend of mine was in the corner drinking hard and telling funny stories.

He got drunker and drunker until at about three in the morning he started shouting and cursing and some glass smashed and finally he fell down. Seeing a dad huddled in a moist heap on our linoleum floor was a great shock. I had never seen a drunken dad before. My dad liked to tell of the three times he had been drunk in his whole life, once in the war and one time with the neighbors and one time in the city, but my brothers and I thought he was probably exaggerating to prove that he was like other dads, which he wasn't, at all.

At the party thirty years ago my friend picked up his crumpled dad, and held him in his arms like a fireman holding a child, and slid grimly along the wall to the door, and propped the door open with his foot, and carried his dad outside. I watched him do this but did nothing to help. I just stood there. Not the first time and not the last that I will stand silent and useless and frozen.

Over the next thirty years I never said a word about that night and neither did my friend. Here and there he would leak a story about a moment when he was a kid and his dad was carried home by the police, or about getting his dad out of the drunk tank, or about the morning his mom changed the locks on their house, or about how his sister went to live with their dad but came home silent a day later, or about how one of the brothers died in a car crash and the father didn't make the funeral, or about how when the dad died finally they put his ashes in a whiskey bottle, but we never talked about that night at the party. All the rest of my life I'll remember my friend's face as he carried his dad in his arms that night, though. I'll never forget that. You think we have words for this sort of thing but we do not. All we can do is witness and report and hope that somehow stories turn into prayers. All we can do is drape words on experience, and hope the words give some hint of the shape of the moment, and pray that our attentiveness matters in a way we will never know. I believe, with all my heart, that it does. What do you believe?

THE TIES THAT BIND

A Vast Table

My first sense that the world might be larger than my street came at an old oaken table, around which my family gathered night after night for meals and musing. Table talk was the necessary glue in my large and opinionated tribe, and many nights after dinner my mother would light a cigarette and hold court, her children ranged around the table in various states of splay, the talk usually political or literary but liable to lurch into education, religion, medicine, morality, or the biochemical workings of the compost heap behind the garage. Each child arrived at an expertise or two over the years, according to taste: my sister talked religion and politics, my older brother politics and mathematics, and my younger brothers sylvology and ichthyology, respectively, although my youngest brother also had a thing for ships and waters, believing, as did the Water Rat in Kenneth Grahame's *The Window in the Willows*, that "there is absolutely nothing half so much worth doing as simply messing about in boats," which he has done ever since, even unto deep-sea diving, and unspooling twine through the silent black caverns of sunken ships as he swims through them.

It was at that table of red oak that I first went abroad: I remember the words *Australia* and *Manila* unspooling in the air, places my father had been in the war, and then *Canada*, much of which he had visited in the course of his work as a journalist. Into the stacks of books surrounding the table I chased the landscapes of that consonantal work, and so discovered further delicious matters to explore — the Yukon, Quebec, Saskatchewan, the works of Mordechai Richler and Robertson Davies, the habits of the mysterious Canadian lynx. This happened again and again, with all sorts of nations, and by the time I actually set foot on foreign soil, years later, I had already traveled widely at home, absorbing not only the first lesson of study abroad, that every culture is different, but my first inkling of the deeper lesson, that all people crave the same foods in their lives: love, substance, grace.

Some years ago my brother the woodman and artisan made a new and larger table for my mother, also red oak, and every summer now the clan gathers around it and sails into the ocean of talk and memory and story that creates and sustains a family through time and across continents. My father and mother anchor their ends of the table, their children and children's children ranged in motley moil between, and thus arrayed we set forth through landscapes strange and wondrous, telling tales as we go, starting a new crew of children on unimaginable journeys of their own, the keel of their imaginations a sturdy oaken table wonderfully larger than it appears to be.

A War Story

My father went to war in March of 1943, just before he was to graduate from Queens College in New York City. An astute and popular young man (he was president of his class), he joined the Army and was sent eventually to aerial intelligence training in Maryland. In October of 1943 he came home on a pass and married my mother. In the summer of 1944 he was made a master sergeant and sent to the Pacific on the troop ship *S.S. Mormacsea*. Neither he nor my mother knew where he was going, and it would be many months before my mother knew that her husband had been assigned to the Americal Division, which had been cut to shreds in battles among the Solomon Islands. The names of two of those islands still chill Pacific veterans: Guadalcanal, Bougainville.

"Because the censorship was so strict, it was many months before I knew where Jim was," wrote my mother recently. By the time she heard from an uncensored husband, he was in Australia, in an Army intelligence unit attached to General Douglas MacArthur's command. As the Pacific war moved into the Philippines, so did my father, and 50 years ago this June he and his unit arrived in Manila. In July he began hearing from Far East Air Force pilots that the war would soon be over. He thought they were crazy. He was working on plans for the invasion of Tokyo on August 6, when an American plane dropped an atomic bomb on Hiroshima.

My father, a photo reconnaissance expert, was among the first men to see B-29 photographs of Hiroshima after the bomb exploded. "It seemed that the city had been obliterated," says my father, who chooses his words carefully. Japan opened peace negotiations August 10, the day after Nagasaki was obliterated. On August 14 Japan accepted surrender terms, and on September 2, in Tokyo Bay, the war ended with a stroke of a pen. Three months later my father boarded the *General John Pope* and came home.

His father, a thoughtful man, had reserved a room at the McAlpin Hotel in New York City for his son, and that is where my father and mother met and resumed their lives in January of 1946. Soon enough another conflict would call, and my father would put his uniform on again, but for the moment his war was over.

He was 24 years old.

The Sea of My Mother

I tell a tale of my mother, from whom all my things flowed, not just once many years ago but ever since, as she is a wise woman, honest, with a discerning eye and a piercing tongue, both fiery and gentle with the headstrong sons she made, four living, one gone ahead, and one daughter, quiet and funny, prayers in her mouth all day long, as she lives in a monastery, and devotes her hours to delving the divine coherence flowing buoyantly beneath us like an ocean on which we are small boats.

My mother's people came to Manhattan on large boats from Counties Clare and Cork and once upon the breast of America they flourished, making the most of the milk and honey that came their way, what little there was of it, as they were laborers and roofers and ostlers and such, and then as the years passed they forced themselves up a notch, to the point where my mother's father wore a white collar as he spent his days clerking. This lad, John Francis Clancey, married Ethel McCluskey, daughter of the seventh son of a seventh son, in a church on 131st Street, and not a year later John Francis and Ethel were back in the church with their first daughter, also named Ethel, and so my mother's blessings began in a brilliant autumn long ago.

She was carried home to the Bronx, to a rural house at the very end of the trolley line, and the clatterclank of train cars rattles all through her life.

She is 16, taking the train to high school in Brooklyn. She is 20, taking the train to Queens College of the City University of New York. She is 22, freshly married, riding the rails to work in the Public Library. Her husband goes to war in the Pacific, he returns, they have a son, the son dies, they are bereft and bereaved, they are living in a cold black country of the heart; but here comes another son, in a terrific snowstorm, and the daughter who will grow up with prayers in her mouth, and then in a rush three more sons, one of whom is far from his mother this evening, and telling this winding tale of her as a prayer, an elegy, a kiss on those lips that kissed me so often, that told so many tales to her blessed boyo.

Not a day goes by when I do not think of her, the woman in whom I lived for nearly a year. Out of seed and blood and joy she made me, carving me to the specifications of the Lord, bringing me forth hours after attending Mass, struggling heavily to her feet from where she knelt in prayer for her about-to-be boy, who would come that afternoon, and be named for Brian Boroimhe, high king, *ard righ*, of Ireland; and many years later he is typing these words, his heart reeling at the way his mother gave her utter self and soul to her children. Whatever I am, she is, until the end of my days, when I shall return to her warm embrace, *ma mére*, the sea from whence I came.

Tangle of Bearberry

My mother is driving me through the rain to the beach. I am applying for summer jobs. The rain is thorough and silvery. We do not speak. The trees along the road are scrubby and gnarled and assaulted by reeds. I am huddled in my jacket. No one else is on the road. You never thank your mother enough. The road is so wet that our tires send up tendrils and spouts of water behind us. I can see them flaring steadily in the mirror on my side. My mother is intent on the road. She would like to say something gentle about the interview I will have in a few minutes but she knows that I will not hear what she says. I will hear what I thought she said, which is not what she said. I heard a lot of what was not said or meant then instead of what was.

My mother woke me that morning, and fed me, and handed me clean folded clothes, and handed me the plethora of forms I was supposed to have filled out but had not filled out and of course filled out hurriedly scribbledly scrawlingly as she drove me through the rain to the beach. We drove along silently as I scribbled and she maybe thought about all the things she would have liked to say but was too wise to say.

This would have been a perfect time for me to say or whisper or even mumble my gratitude to my mother for eighteen years of extraordinary love and care. This would have been a great time for me to say something like I see your hard work, mom, and I see your weariness with all these kids, and I see how quietly worried you and dad are about money, and I can only faintly dimly imagine what it must be like to bear and coddle and raise and protect and educate and love children and have them be rude and vulgar and dismissive and contemptuous and worse. That would have been a great time for me to say something gentle for once. Rarely were we alone together for thirty minutes as we were that morning in the rain on the road to the beach.

That would have been a great time for me to say quietly I see you, mom, and I love you, and I never say that, and I should say that every thirty seconds every blessed day, and I should touch my head to the holy earth every dawn and say thank you for you to whatever it is that we mean when we say The Mercy and the Coherence and The Imagination. That would have been the perfect time, alone in the quiet car in the quiet rain on the silent road among the gnarled little trees.

By the time we got to the state park headquarters it was too late for me to say anything, and I hurried off to the interview, and I don't know what my mother did for the next few minutes. Probably she went for a walk along the boardwalk, or sat in the car writing letters; she was always in motion, always quietly doing something even in moments when nothing needs to be done; that was how she was and still is, though now she moves very slowly indeed and does not drive at all. Now I drive, and she sits in the passenger seat, and we talk freely and cheerfully and deeply and avidly and eagerly and every time I talk to her I say I love you. We don't say that enough. We don't. After a while I came back from the interview and she started the car and we drove home through the ranks of the bent twisted little trees. There were pitch pines and salt cedars, and here and there beach plums, and thickets of sumac, and I thought I saw a tangle of bearberry but I could not be sure.

Miller's Folly

My father-in-law is buried on a hillside out in the country. Around his headstone are cedar and spruce trees; near him sleeps his grandson, who died young. At the bottom of the hill there is a creek which wends south and east, toward Molalla.

In Molalla is the house he built himself. Before there was a house there were blackberry thickets higher than a man's head. To get to the nearby creak you had to bring a sickle. The house took some years to build because he built it on Saturdays and Sundays. There were several porches and a fireplace big enough to roast a bear. He laid in gardens, lawns, hedges, trees. Because the creek is too shallow for swimming, he dug a pond near it. It would be a cozy swimming hole, he told his wife. He set to work with his sons and grandsons. They dug the hole and cleared away the mud. Instantly the pond filled with frogs and mud. They lugged the froggy mud away with streaming shovels. The pond immediately filled up again. This went on for some years. The pond acquired a family name: Miller's Folly.

Then he died, the house was sold, the family scattered, years passed, I married his final daughter. I went to look at the pond, to find some of the man. It was late afternoon, when the edges of the day turn russet. The pond broke my heart. It is ragged and rife with weeds. Blackberry tangles are everywhere. Cattails obscure the western rim. I stood for a moment watching bright swallows carving rich dusk.

In my mind I told him this was folly; to strive for clarity year after year is madness. He answered me patiently, using his hands to show me the shape of his ambition. His hands were gnarled and deliberate. A mosquito landed on his forehead. His huge ears were silhouetted against the fading light.

I think his soul is here where he fought the mud. I think he is also in the voices of children. I think he is not dead, but coursing through water and dreaming in the hearts of green things. I think that stories summon and honor him, and that tales of him are prayers of enormous power.

Also I think his muddy pond is a sacred place.

The most interesting and powerful sentence ever said to me was terse and spoken on a hill over the sea by a slight stunning woman: *Yes,* she said, firmly, and off we went to be married.

Since then I have become a student of her taut sentences, which are always riveting. *I like to do the dishes because it's order amid disorder,* that was one of my favorites, and *if beavers are smart, we should be worried,* which absorbed me for weeks, and *strong emotion is the only defense against dangerous complacency,* which is true, and *color stole my heart,* which is also true, but lately it is her sentences having to do with her paintings that fascinate me, two in particular, both having to do with the color blue. *The bluer they got, the longer they got,* she said of the legs of a child in one of her paintings, a remark I chewed on for a long time, and then, airily, *I used to be into yellow but lately I've been into blue,* which made me think of blue as a riff, a meal, a country.

So much more than a color, blue — a mood, a music, a tonal sadness, oceanic, riverine, airy, the color of carefree and of holy cloaks, the true color of blood and curses, the color of the calm Jewish teenager who held in her dewy womb a son, an Idea, a death foretold, a murder she would be forced to watch, craning her neck to watch him sag and bleed, one of a thousand crucifixions that foul afternoon, one of a billion since, and how many millions of mothers have wept over the pale bodies of their dead children?

She was a child herself when the vision came and her belly filled with mystery, and who she was really, deep in her heart, is as lost now as her husband's character, the two of them long ago turned to symbol, their blood leached away and replaced with legend. But she bore that Child and loved him dearly, and the wonder-weave of her patience comes untorn through the years; so it is that when we think of the holiness of women and mothers we think of her, wrapped in her blue cloak, smiling against loss and horror and death, and against those savage inevitable wounds we so often whisper not to Him but to her, and isn't that odd and wonderful? that so often so many so desperately dream of a calm Jewish girl whose whole life was a river of *yes?*

Turquoise, cobalt, cerulean, ultramarine, azure, cyanine, hyacinth, indigo, smalt, wistaria: I watch the blues under my wife's paintbrush, I savor the high-beam blue flash of her eyes, I listen, I watch the cat-grace of women and girls, I think of the Jewish girl, I think: *holy holy holy holy holy.*

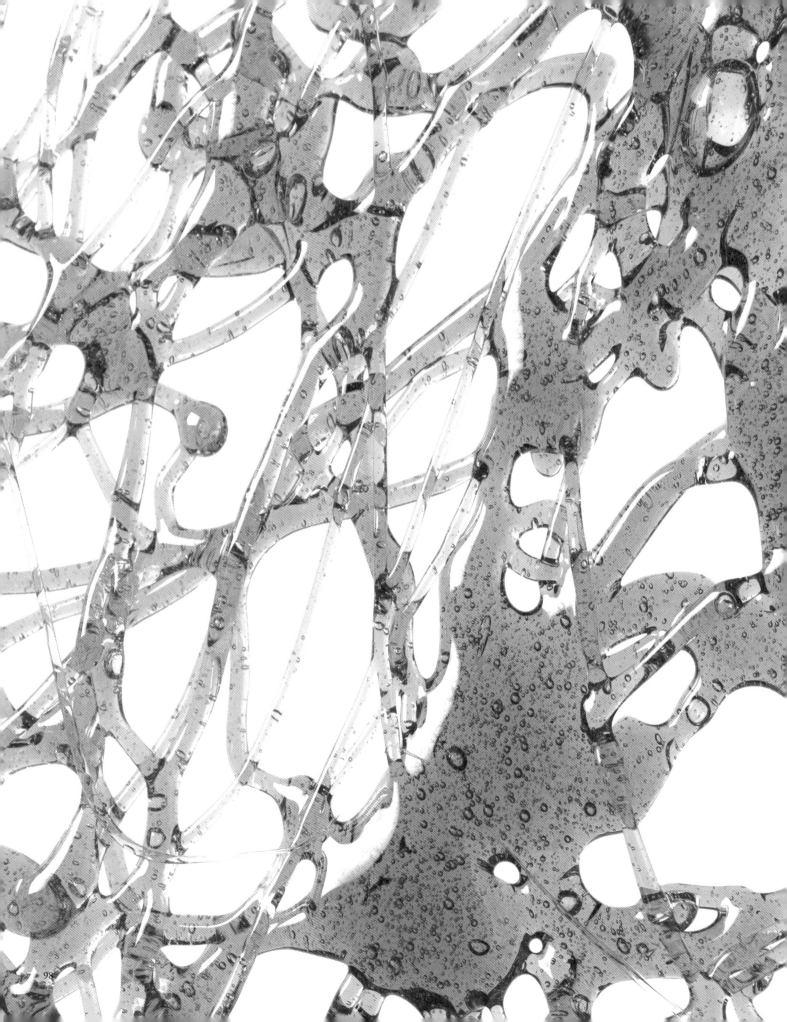

The Ties That Bind

In my house, which is small and white and wooden, there is a shrew, a woman, a man, a girl, an orange tree, two baby boys, nine spiders, a flock of fruit flies, and several dozen honey ants, the remnants of several hundred who until very recently lived in the basement and made regular forays in orderly lines up the stairs and into the kitchen, where they fastidiously held out for honey and jelly, and refused adamantly the spoonfuls of peanut butter so generously proferred them by my daughter, who enjoyed their company, and who took to laying thin lines of honey across the kitchen in lovely patterns, including once a portrait of her father, who watched, awed, daughter in lap, as the lines of his face were populated slowly by ants hardly bigger than bits of sand.

This bit of sweet theater made me think uncomfortably of the way that my face will some-day be a highway for invertebrates when my body is no longer animated by the odd spirit that drives it today, but it also led me to ponder the ways in which my house is a thriving community of creatures, invited and uninvited, all dining on my dollar. Some are there by accident; the shrew fell through an open basement window and landed foursquare on a copy of Edward Gibbon's *The Decline and Fall of the Roman Empire,* which dazed the shrew, to the surprise of no one who has worked upstream against the cascade of Gibbonian sentences. Others, like the spiders and the boys, were born there, and have known no other home, and occasionally share the same diet, specifically beetles, which the boys are wonderfully quick at downing, to the dismay, I assume, of the spiders, not to mention the beetles.

Thus we are bound by humor and beetles, by honey and spider-silk, and by universal astonishment at the shrew, which could not be tamed, but was turned out into the yard to thin the herds of crickets, which it did with wonderful dispatch, that being the nature of shrews. As it scrabbled away into the brush I felt a pang of loss, for it had been one of us, a stitch in the fabric of our family; and I thought, not for the first time, that we are each threaded to each other by love, thorough or insufficient, inexplicable and necessary, as ephemeral and savory as lines of honey, as lines on the face of God.

FATHER
FATHER
FATHER

Making the Bed

I am kneeling on the oak floor, hammering pine. My twin sons' twin beds have been delivered to the house by a humming man with braces. The beds are in many pieces. My wife and daughter and I must piece the beds together tonight, so that the boys, already poured into their pajamas, can hit their respective sacks.

My sons are nearly three years old and the time has come for Big Boy Beds. The Boys are poking each other with screwdrivers, losing the dowels for the beds, tearing the plastic covers off the mattresses, etc. My daughter, six years old, capable with tools and proud of it, is cheerfully screwing the wrong screw in the wrong hole in the wrong plank; but she does so with such diligence, with such concentrated chewing of tongue and cold-eyed appraisal of screw-depth in screw-hole, with such thoughtful arrangement of large muscles upon small tool, such large joy in small task, that for once I hold my own tongue, and do not scold, or correct, or instruct, or lecture, or seek to edit her activities, but lean back on my haunches and watch.

My wife, a subtle woman, also watches in silence.

My daughter, absorbed, doesn't notice us watching.

She pauses in her labors, considers the tool in hand, lays it down, chooses another, sets to work.

I stare at her face. She's lean and long now, her baby fat long gone, her face brown from the summer.

It's been a tough summer — she's been rebellious, angry, quick to tattoo her brothers with her fists and feet, quick to bark and snap at her mother, to snarl at her father. Perhaps she is nervous about looming kindergarten; but perhaps too she is twisting the wrong way, growing not toward light but toward darkness. I worry about this daily. The rituals of her early years have slipped away, but nothing yet has replaced them; sometimes we read together sweetly and she folds into me like a new rib but mostly now we don't, and often now we are sharp with each other, our voices have cutting edges, doors slam. Often I sit on the edge of the jail chair and try to explain my reasoning and she turns away, she says *I don't care,* she says *I hate you,* she says *are you finished yet?*

And often I sit there when she has stomped off and think *what have I done wrong?*

I think maybe people of grace and courage and honesty are made like Big Boy Beds — piece by piece, slowly, with a lot of kneeling. I think maybe parents, despite appearances, haven't the slightest idea how to bring up their children, but simply keep at it with as much kindness as they can summon to the work. I think maybe we are making our children's beds all day long, year after year, until suddenly the child in the bed is a woman kneeling on another floor in another city making a bed for her child, and even then you don't stop making her bed, but lend a hand with the new bed too. So there is no end to the making of beds, including your own.

My daughter finishes her work and smiles broadly. We smile broadly. The boys, smiling broadly, hit each other with hammers. Some minutes later, in my appointed paternal editing rounds, I come upon the wrong screw in the wrong hole, but for once I do not seek to correct a flaw, because it seems to me now that it is actually the right screw in the right hole, and we all build the rest of the bed, and although in the weeks to come my sons will continue to sleep curled on the floor as they always have, that particular bed seems like a wonderfully well-made bed to me.

The Measure of Mystery

My daughter and I are in the habit of reclining together in the gathering twilight, in her small room at the top of the stairs, in the last russet half-hour before she closes up shop for the night. Once we are settled, coverlets and bears just so, there is the traditional paternal quiz (*how was your day, did you have fun, where did you go?*), the traditional daughterly replies (*fine, yes, out*), and the now-traditional paternal musing, there in the sifting dust of dusk, about the utterly mysterious interior life of my oldest child, once a fixed entity the size of a shoebox, and now a long-legged unpredictability, Almost Six Years Old.

For some years now the last voice in Lily's ear every night has been her father's baritone mutter, the guttural mumble of a man making his way through the published adventures of trolls, pigs, mice, otters, wolves, and ballerinas. Some months ago we began a series of invented tales about foxes, a story-cycle that stars a small gray fox (*urocyon cinereoargenteus*) named Phil, who found his way into school one day, and stayed, a furry phenomenon in the last row. At our fictional Fox Hollow School there are quizzes every Friday morning, and lately it has been Friday morning every night, as Lily has become absorbed by tests: science tests, spelling tests, math tests. Perhaps what she loves is the sense of accomplishment that comes with correct answers to questions like *how do you spell door?* or *name three foods that a bear eats,*

or perhaps the startled pride in her father's gravelly compliment when his small student solves a conundrum like *what is 11 minus 9 plus 4?* Or perhaps it is simply that she loves the challenge, loves to measure her mind against mystery.

And lately, in that last lovely light, with that light lovely head on my chest, I have been mesmerized by the mystery of her mind. How do you solve *what's 11 minus 7?* I asked her the other night. Easy, she said: ten, one; nine, two; eight, three; seven, four; so the answer is four.

I puzzled over this for a minute until I saw the pattern, the moving of stones from one pile to another, and then lay there silent, overcome with the gift that had been given to me: the chance to watch a new mind flowering — and a mind, to boot, that I had begged the Lord for, ferociously, my fists hammering on His door night after night, until unto me there was born a daughter, a new note in the long song of the world, a story who will be told, I pray, long after I have myself become sifting dust at dusk. In the leap of her mind there is a miracle so startling that I am but a stuttering student of it, a small boy peering between the blinds, a child struggling to sense the Coherence in everything, and sometimes, just before nightfall, in a small room with a small girl, I do.

Pop

In nine years I have been graced with three children and here is what I have learned about their species. They are engines of incalculable joy and agonizing despair. They are comedy machines. Their language is their own and the order of their new halting words has never been heard before in the whole history of the world. They are headlong and hilarious. Their hearts are enormous and sensitive beyond calculation by man or machine. Their pride is vast. Their energy is unflagging. They are cruel, and move in herds and gaggles and mobs, and woe unto the silent one, the one who looks funny, the one who speaks awkwardly, the fat one, for she will be shouldered aside, he will never get the ball, she will never be asked to jump rope, he will not be invited to the pool party, she will weep with confusion and rage, he will lash out with sharp small fists. Yet they are endlessly kind, kind by nature, and among them there is often an artless democracy, a linking of arms against the vast puzzle of the long people. They search for rules and rank, for what is allowed and what is forbidden, and poke the rules to see which bends and which is steel, for they wish to know

Art

their place in the world, where they might walk, what they may wear, which shows are allowed, how far they can go, who they are. They rise early in excitement and return reluctantly to barracks at night for fear of missing a shred of the daily circus. They grow at stunning rates that produce mostly leg. They are absorbed by dogs. Mud accrues to them. Once they learn sarcasm they use it with abandon, slashing here and there recklessly and wreaking havoc. When they weep they weep utterly from the marrows of their lonely bones. They do not speak of death but when that dark hawk comes they face him without fear. They are new creatures hourly, and what you think you know of them is wrong. They know far more than you think they know. When they are ill they shrivel. To father them is not a brief noun but an endless verb that exhausts, enrages, edifies, elevates, educates; I am a grayer man than I was, and worn with worries; and closer to joy. They awe me, for they will make a new world on the buckled back of the one I love; but they delight me, for to love them is to taste the capacious love the Maker has for what He fathered, and fathers still, and always will.

Chessay

My son asked me to play chess yesterday. When a child asks you to play chess you say yes. He is twenty years old and an excellent chess player. I taught him to play when he was five years old. He first beat me when he was thirteen years old. What I remember best from that day is his slow smile when he and I realized, a few moves before the end, that he had toppled the king. I remember too that he did not crow or caper or shout or cackle but instead reached across the board and shook my hand, as I taught him to do, out of respect for the game, and for your opponent, in whose mind you have been swimming for an hour. Chess at its best is a deeply intimate game in which you can delve into another person's mind and if you are lucky you get a glance a hint an intimation of your opponent's character and creativity, the cast of his mind, the flare of her personality, how he confronts difficulties, how rash or calm she is, how willing to be surprised, how well he loses, how poorly she wins.

He came out along his left wing, immediately establishing his knights, immediately forcing me to scuffle and skitter around on defense. My queen roared off her throne snarling and forced her way all the way to his back line but he deftly boxed her in with yapping pawns. Sometimes I think the pawn is the most powerful piece of all. Revolutions and religions begin with ragged beggars from the wilderness. I sent my bishops slicing here and there. My pawns grappled and died. He missed one golden fatal chance with a knight. The knight's curious sidelong move is the deepest genius of chess; it is the one piece that does not move in linear fashion, the one piece with a geometry of its own, the piece that goes its own way, the mystical piece.

In a moment he will be thirty. I want to stare at him across the board for a week. He catches me in a mistake that takes me forever to redress. I don't know how to say any words that would catch the way I love him. I want him to outwit me. I want to win and I want to lose and I want to savor how deftly I am defeated. I often wonder if I have been a good enough father. A good father teaches his son how to kill the king. He makes an infinitesimal mistake and my rooks close in grimly. I have prayed desperately to die before he does. I would like to teach his children to play chess. I would like to show them how, if you are lucky, you can see inside your opponent, only occasionally, only dimly, only for a few minutes, but for those few minutes you get a hint an intimation a glance at who lives inside the castle of his body. What we see of each other is only a bit of who we are. I want to invent new words for what we mean when we say the word love. Chess can be a wonderful word for that. Chess is a lovely word that can't be spoken. After the game we shake hands and I think never in the history of the world was there ever a man happier to be a father than me. Never in the whole long bristling history of the world.

Illuminos

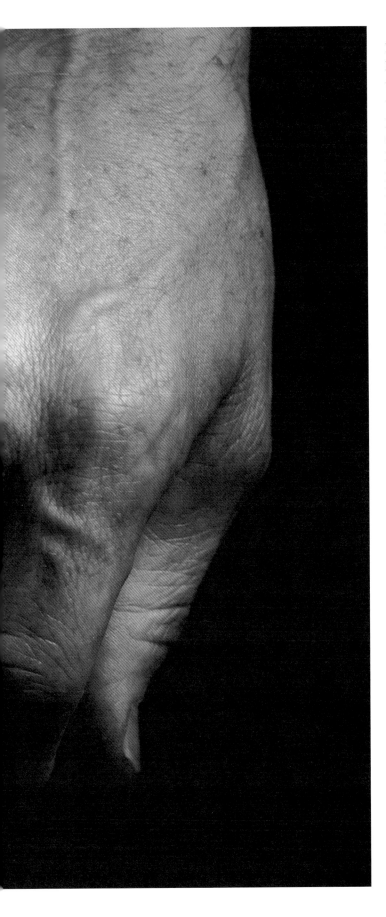

One child held onto my left pinky finger everywhere we went.
Never any other finger and never the right pinky but only the
left pinky and never my whole hand. My finger misses her hand
this morning. It has been many years since she held my finger. To
this day sometimes in the morning when I dress I stare at my left
pinky and suddenly I am in the playground, or on the beach, or in
a thrumming crowd, and there is a person weighing forty pounds
holding onto my left pinky so tightly that I am tacking slightly to
port. I miss tacking slightly to port. Another child held onto my
left trouser leg most of the time but he would, if he deemed it
necessary, hold either of my hands, and one time both of my
hands, when we were shuffling in the surf, and the water was up
to my knees but up to his waist, and I walked along towing him
like a small grinning chortling dinghy all the way from the sea
cave where we thought there might be sea lions sleeping off a
salmon bender to the tidepools where you could find starfish and
crabs and anemones and mussels the size of your shoes.

The third child held my hands happily all the time, either hand,
any hand, my hands, his mother's hands, his brother's hands,
his sister's hands, his friends, aunts and uncles and cousins and
grandparents and teachers, dogs and trees, neighbors and bushes,
he would hold hands with any living creature whatsoever,
without the slightest trepidation or self-consciousness, and to
this day I admire that boy's open genuine eager unadorned verve.
He once held hands with his best friend during an entire soccer
game when they were five years old, the two of them running
in tandem, or one starting in one direction unbeknownst to the
other and down they both went giggling in the sprawl of the
grass. It seems to me that angels and bodhisattvas are everywhere
available for consultation if only we can see them clear; they are
unadorned, and joyous, and patient, and radiant, and luminous,
and not disguised or hidden or filtered in any way whatsoever, so
that if you see them clearly, which happens occasionally even to
the most blinkered and frightened of us, you realize immediately
who they are, beings of great and humble illumination dressed in
the skins of new and dewy beings, and you realize, with a catch in
your throat, that they are your teachers, and they are agents of an
unimaginable love, and they are your cousins and companions in
awe, and they are miracles and prayers and songs of inexplicable
beauty whom no one can explain and no one own or claim or
trammel, and that simply to perceive them is to be blessed beyond
the reach of language, and that to be the one appointed to tow
them along a beach, or a crowd, or home through the brilliant
morning from the muddy hilarious peewee soccer game, is to be
graced beyond measure or understanding; which is what I was,
and I am, and I will be, until the day I die, and change form from
this one to another, in ways miraculous and mysterious, never to
be plumbed by the mind or measures of man.

MERE
MIRROR

A Ferocious Curiosity

I do not remember that science ever riveted me as a boy; my early obsessions in life were basketball and books, and then came the hurricanes of puberty, during which my mind worked fitfully, if at all. Science in college was something to survive, and after college my interests were basketball, young ladies, books, whiskey, and employment, in approximately that order.

It wasn't until I was in my roaring twenties that I snapped awake fully to the intricate and miraculous machinery of the natural world. I remember what woke me up, too — a marsh hawk that sliced past me one day as I was driving beside the ocean. It was a male with smoke-gray wings. He cut sharply in front of my car and dropped onto a meadow vole, a common mouse of the flat coastal lands where I grew up. I flew by this scene at 40 miles an hour but the drama of it has stayed with me ever since: the hawk's perfect timing, the buffeting of his wings as he exchanged air for earth, the limp sag of the mouse caged in those razor-fingers.

I was hooked, after that. I had suddenly *seen* a bird closely, seen it as an individual creature, seen a chapter of its story. I began to pay attention to the fluttering creatures around me, and once my eyes were opened the immense variety of the bird world rushed in relentlessly. They were everywhere I turned, in a bewildering array of shapes, sizes, colors, styles of survival. Since my epiphany on the highway I have become a serious student of birds, particularly hawks; in a manner of speaking I have become an amateur scientist — a hawkist, perhaps, or a raptorophiliac.

In the course of my bird studies I have met many Real Scientists — ornithologists, physiologists, naturalists, biologists, male and female, old and young. I respect them enormously. They are people driven by an immense curiosity; in some way they have not lost the itchy need-to-know of children, and this makes them jumpy and wonderful people whom I greatly admire and whose ferocious curiosity is infectious. Such infection has greatly improved me; I think it is a rare case in which a disease has been of great benefit to the patient.

First Day

When I went to college I carried a battered old green canvas duffel bag. My dad had stenciled my name on it in white paint at his basement work-bench. The old black steamer trunk had been shipped ahead of me and it was waiting in the basement of my hall and I remember hauling it up the steps to my room just like a man would haul a recalcitrant walrus, with all his might and with no help whatsoever from the walrus. Other guys were hauling their trunks to their rooms also, and one older guy offered to help me, and I will always remember his face because he was the first person to help me on my first day at college even though he didn't know me at all and I was only a freshman. The hallway smelled like wood chips and paint and turpentine and the shaggy musty dank of rooms being opened and aired after being shut tight all through the roaring American summer. My room was small but tall and I claimed the bottom bunk and the desk by the window and unpacked my stuff and then my roommate walked in. He was from Missouri and he carried a banjo. I had never seen a banjo before and said so and he said he would play it a lot which he subsequently did, sometimes at dawn, which was a mixed blessing.

He went off with his family, and I sat at my desk for a while fidgeting and pinning up photographs of my family and then even though I should have made the effort to be friendly and meet the other guys on my floor, or review my class schedule for the hundredth time, or hit the bookstore to get a running head start on syllabi, I did none of these things, for I was rattled and frightened and near tears for reasons I did not know, so I opened my

old black trunk and got out my worn gleaming basketball and slipped out of the hall without saying anything to anyone and ran down toward the lake where I knew there were basketball courts because my brother had told me about them. He had been a student at this college also years ago and when he was lonely and rattled he went to the lake. Some-how having my ball in my hands and spinning on my fingers and whipping around my back on the dribble and bouncing between my legs occasion-ally was soothing and nutritious. Who would have ever thought that bouncing a basketball for an hour would be the mysterious food you needed at exactly that hour in your life? But it was so, and I shot baskets and ran through my ancient mindless drills for an hour there by the small glistening lake, with its fringe of reeds like a prickly fence between land and water, and when I was done, when I was dripping and tired and something sad had been burned away, I hit a last shot, because you can never never never leave a court without hitting your last shot, and then I dipped my hands in the lake and splashed my face and walked slowly back to my hall. On the way back people on the pathways smiled and said hey, and I smiled and mumbled, and when I got to my hall two older students on the steps said hey and asked me my name and shook my hand, and one of the older students said hey man grab me tomorrow and we'll get some guys and run full-court down by the lake. I said okay, sure, thanks, great, thanks, and I walked down the hall to my room feeling some kind of different, like maybe just maybe things would be some kind of okay.

A Tour of the Continent

When I was a sophomore in college, very many years ago, I had a chance to spend a year in Ireland. I had never been to Ireland, and itched to go; my family was proudly Irish as far back as we could trace, and I had been soaked in Irish literature and lore and song since I was an elf. I even knew some Irish—a string of Gaelic oaths so foul that they peeled paint off walls and felled birds from the sky, oaths I'd learned from my gentle grandmother, who was given to exclaiming in Gaelic when she lost her temper, which was, all things considered, fairly often, God rest her soul. She was a very fine woman afflicted with grandsons and cats.

I applied to the program. I scribbled all night filling out the forms, I composed a piercing essay explaining my itch for Eire, I slid the packet under an office door at dawn. A week later my roommate tossed a letter up to the top bunk; it was my acceptance notice. I whooped, I hollered, I called my parents, I bought maps of the Republic, I bought a pair of sturdy walking boots for mucking about the auld sod.

But I didn't go. The more I thought about a year abroad, the more I regretted the loss of a year with my roommates, my friends, my family. After much chewing of fingernails I wrote a letter declining the position. My father was aghast at this decision, my mother startled and displeased. My roommates were puzzled; why would I want to stay with *them*?

I finally made it to Ireland, ten years later, and the experience was hilarious and muddy and poignant. Yet more than once in my time there I thought of the year abroad I did not have, and regretted its loss, because I have come to think that breadth is the greatest gift we can give youth, and a year abroad would have been good for the shy boy I was then. To be soaked in another culture is a wonderful way to prevent hubris; in fact it is, as that very fine essayist William Hazlitt noted, a way in which "lessons might be learned in other languages, and provincialism pared away as if it was a bruise on fruit, which is all the more savory for the excision."

MARY DAVERN
WIFE OF PATRICK
DIED

Other Oregons

This past summer I attended the Fourth of July parade in Neskowin, Oregon. It is a very small parade: a fire engine, an elderly jazz band, a number of residents dressed as political or literary figures, excited children on bicycles, yowling dogs, a phlegmatic horse, and a man wearing a suit made of tin cans.

The parade winds around the village once and ends up at the grocery store, where there are speeches and songs and awards. Every year I stand there and sing the songs I know: "The Star Spangled Banner," "You're a Grand Old Flag," "God Bless America." I do not know the Marine and Army Air Corps anthems and so do not sing them. Nor, until recently, did I know the words to "Oregon, My Oregon," which concludes matters with a stately flourish.

Every year, as I hear the many voices around me quavering the state song, I think about Oregon. I did not grow up here and so I had wild ideas of the place: beavers the size of cars, oceans of rain, gargantuan fir forests blanketing the state. Then I came here to live, and discovered other Oregons: salt-sprayed, dry-dust, African, Suislawan, Japanese, Vietnamese, Kalapuyan. One Oregon is indeed moist and green and covered with trees of herculean girth; another is a pitted moonscape of smoldering slash piles; a third is a vast high sage desert. One is a booming techno-society fueled by espresso and alert to social, cultural, and environmental concerns; another is populated by starving migrant children. One is the face of an owl chick nailed to a television pole; another is the harrowed face of the madwoman who wanders through my town carrying her possessions in a tattered Safeway bag; still others are the faces of my friends and family, whose graces are universities to me.

Last summer, feeling grateful to Oregon for the peace and zest and children I have been given here, I learned the words to the state song. I sang them awkwardly and off-key and, to my utter surprise, with tears streaming into my beard.

Land of the rose and sunshine,
Land of the summer's breeze;
Laden with health and vigor
Fresh from the Western seas,
Blest by the blood of martyrs,
Land of the setting sun;
Hail to thee, Land of Promise,
My Oregon.

Love, Bone, Fury

I teach occasionally, not well, haltingly, in a rumbling nasal mumble, with a tendency to speak too fast and wave my arms in an alarming manner and shift recklessly from topic to topic like a man desperate to find the right gear in a borrowed car. I rant and rave and slide suddenly into anecdotes that often feature my hilarious daughter and melon-headed twin sons. I cannot go five minutes (or three sentences) without making reference to the genius poet William Blake. I wring my hands and stutter and mutter and recite shreds of poetry. Once, in the cracked guttural voice of a toad, I sang a song. I ask students sudden personal questions. I sail off into disquisitions about George Orwell and Flannery O'Connor and Li Po. I begin by talking quietly about writing, which is an ancient and muscular art, and end by talking passionately about love and bone and fury, because those things are in the very best writing.

As I shuffle toward the class I am to teach I always think darkly that I have nothing to say, because fine writing is hard to explain; it is made by terrific labor, rude honesty, and the irresistible urge to tell stories. But then I am in front of the class and I start to tell stories, among which is the incredibly persistent story of a young Jewish carpenter hammered to a wooden cross and murdered and reborn, and of Gautama Buddha, who sat like a root under a tree for a year before he saw the intricate weave of the world, and of the Irish genius Van Morrison, who sings the truth, and of Cú Chulainn mac Súaltaim and Finn mac Cumaill, the roaring heroes of ancient Ireland, and of my friend Blake, who saw angels bespangled in trees and who spoke to the prophet Elijah on Saturdays, and of my wife and children, whose love and stories sustain and save me, and the hour flies by and I have to be wrestled from the classroom by burly deans.

As I shuffle back to my office, my brain humming, I think three things: that the essence of teaching is the passing of enthusiasm to students; that the courtesy of students is, thank God, immense; and that the greatest virtue of education is that it is relentless, it comes always, often unexpectedly, often unbidden, sometimes from muttering middle-aged men with bent noses and bad ties, who mill their arms and sing their delight like children open-mouthed in the sudden summer rain.

One Minute Ago
Twenty Years Ago
One Minute Ago

Was driving past my children's grade school the other day and started to laugh, thinking of all the entertaining and hectic and chaotic and hilarious moments our children had enjoyed there, and I pulled over behind the school, where the muddy field and wood-chipped playground and moist basketball court and dense fringe of forest all crowd together with their edges spilling over gently so that moss marks the boundaries of the court and hawthorn trees finger the field, and I wandered around remembering stuff.

In my experience, if you wander around long enough with your reasoning software disabled, you might be plunged back thrillingly through time, and find yourself grinning as you watch your small daughter do soccer drills in the mud, and your elfin sons playing wall-ball with a ball very nearly as large as they are, and your tiny daughter swinging so high on the swings that you quietly position yourself to make the catch of a lifetime if necessary, and your headlong sons thrashing through the under-story picking blackberries, and your exuberant daughter leaping from Utah to Ohio on the huge painted map of the United States on the pathway, and your grinning sons taking heroic cuts at a stationary baseball perched innocently on a tee, and your shy daughter and sons holding your right hand as you walk them up the hill to kindergarten, and bringing them their forgotten lunches, and looking all over the field and playground for lost jackets and hats and gloves and sweaters and basketballs and shin-pads, and a thousand other moments like that, all floating in the misted air over the scraggly field and along the uneven pathway and among the snowberries in the fringes of the forest.

They rocketed along on their bicycles and flung footballs and hatched conspiracies and gazed tongue-tied at girls and ran in packs and troops and gaggles. They played every sort of game most of which I will never know. They were scratched and bruised here and they sliced open their knees and elbows here and they bled here and surely they wept here and I know for a fact they laughed so helplessly here that their cheeks and stomachs hurt from laughing. There were field days and carnivals and picnics and assemblies and lines of burbling children ambling back into the school in that wonderfully motley way that lines of children move, two or three kids in cadence and then the next two gawking at a hawk and the ones behind them shoving and the next bent over tying his shoelace and the next kid trips over him and there is a pileup and the teacher at the back of the line says hey! and in a minute it will start to rain so incredibly hard that kids inside will press their faces against the windows in awe and leave perfect fading circles of their holy and magical breath.

I saw and felt and heard all these things as real and powerful and immediate and tender as the instant they happened ten years ago fifteen years twenty years ago and I wanted to weep and laugh at the same time and I had to go sit down on the swing where my daughter was swinging one minute ago twenty years ago one minute ago. The swing was rocking ever so gently when I went to sit down on it, and you might say it was the wind, or a flicker of breeze from a heron walloping by overhead, or the butterfly effect, whereby a small change in one state of a deterministic nonlinear system can result in large differences in a later state, but you know and I know that my daughter had just leapt off the swing to run giggling through the tunnel of immense truck tires, and the swing still felt her slight weight, and always will.

What Matters

Hawks huddled disgruntled against hissing snow. Wrens in winter thickets. Swallows carving and swimming and slicing fat grinning summer air. Frozen dew outlining every single blade of grass. Salmonberries blackberries thimbleberries raspberries cloudberries snowberries strawberries blueberries gooseberries. My children learning to read. The sinuous liquid flow of rivers and minks and cats. Fresh bread with waaay too much butter. My children's hands when they cup my ancient grizzled face in their hands. Exuberance and ebullience. Tears of sorrow which are the salt sea of the heart. Sleep in every form from doze to bone-weary. The shivering ache of a saxophone and the yearning of an oboe. Folding laundry hot from the dryer. Cobblers and tailors. A spotless kitchen floor. The way horses smell in spring. Postcards on which the sender has written so much that he or she can barely squeeze in a signature. Opera on the radio. Toothbrushes. The postman's grin. The green sifting powdery snow of cedar pollen on my porch every year. The way a heron labors through the sky with such vast elderly dignity. People who care about hubcaps. The cheerful ears of dogs. All photographs of every sort. Tip-jars. Wineglasses. The way barbers sweep up circles of hair after haircuts. Handkerchiefs. Libraries. Poems read aloud by older poets. Fedoras. Excellent knives. The very *idea* of albatrosses. Thesaurii. The tiny screws that hold spectacles together. Book marginalia done with the lightest possible pencil. People who keep dead languages alive. Wooden rulers. Fresh-mown lawns. First-basemen's mitts. Dishracks. The way my sons smell after their baths. The moons of Jupiter, especially Io. All manner of boats. The fact that our species produced Edmund Burke. Naps of every size. Junior Policemen badges. Walrussssses. Cassocks and surplices. The orphaned caps of long-lost pens. Welcome-mats and ice-cream trucks. All manner of bees. Cabbages and kings. Eulogy and elegy and puppetry. Fingernail-clippers. The rigging of sailing ships. Ironing-boards. Hoes and scythes. The mysterious clips that girls wear in their hair. Bodhisattvas and beauticians. Porters and portmanteaus. Camas and canvas. Bass and bluefish. Furriers and farriers. Trout and grout. Peach pies of any size. The sprawling porches of old hotels and the old men who sprawl upon them. The snoring of children. The burble of owls. The sound of my daughter typing her papers for school in the other room. The sound of my sons wrangling and wrestling and howling and yowling. All sounds of whatever tone and tenor issuing from my children. My children, and all other forms of coupled pain and joy; which is to say everything alive; which is to say all prayers; which is what I am doing.

STONE
OVER
BONE

Almost

Maybe they're all alive, that's what I keep thinking. All of them — the children who died during pregnancy, the stillborn, the infants who died suddenly in their sleep, the toddlers who died in every conceivable manner, the millions and millions and millions of children who are aborted.

Almost-people.

Sometimes I dream that they live in cities of their own, and that they have all reached a certain age — fifteen, say. All those almost-children now sprouted to lanky boys and willowy girls, as shy and flirty and confused and eager as any teen-agers. They do the same things that teenagers who are alive do — skateboards and cars and trying to look cool and smoking cigarettes and making out in movie theaters and homework and nervous fumbling hormones on moldy creaking basement couches and arguing and basketball and pimples and being terrified and thrilled at what might happen to them when they are women and men.

My dream never gets into the details of how they shape their loneliness. I just see them, is all, and wonder why we don't talk about them. They seem real to me. They're just quiet.

I am a man, and know nothing of the hearts of women, but their mothers never forget the times when children were riding under their bellies between their hipbones, do they? A mother never forgets an abortion, does she?, even if it was early, even if it was the right thing, wasn't it?, she's said that to herself so many times that it has become the right thing, and no amount of inane political chatter or insipid religious rant can change her mind, for she lives in the rightness of that act, survives in the sliver of it being possibly the right thing.

Wasn't it?

But she doesn't forget the heavy feeling in her abdomen and then the feeling of the heavy feeling gone.

The earth groans with people, more than ever before on the planet, and more coming, and aquifers falling, and children starving, and more to starve in the years to come, and pollution rampant, and a hole opening through which the icy dark of space pours in, and new diseases rage into the population, and we kill every creature we see and those we don't see, and we argue about the number of children we should have, and contraception, and tax breaks, and genetic engineering first of plants and now of us, and we talk about zero population, and argue and argue and argue, and meanwhile the number of people booms, and we grow ever more crowded and tense and hungry, and ever more divided into the angry poor and the frightened rich, and in the midst of all this shouting about life and rights and groaning planets, I still dream about the people who almost were.

It doesn't make sense. They're dead. There's no room for them. There's nothing I can do for them but pray, and who knows what good that will do them in their thin country, their transparent country, their country made of glass and whispers?

Nor do I have anything of political or moral muscle to say, no speech, no rant, no web site for you to visit, no cause to which you should send money.

I just see them sometimes. I wonder who they would have been. Don't you?

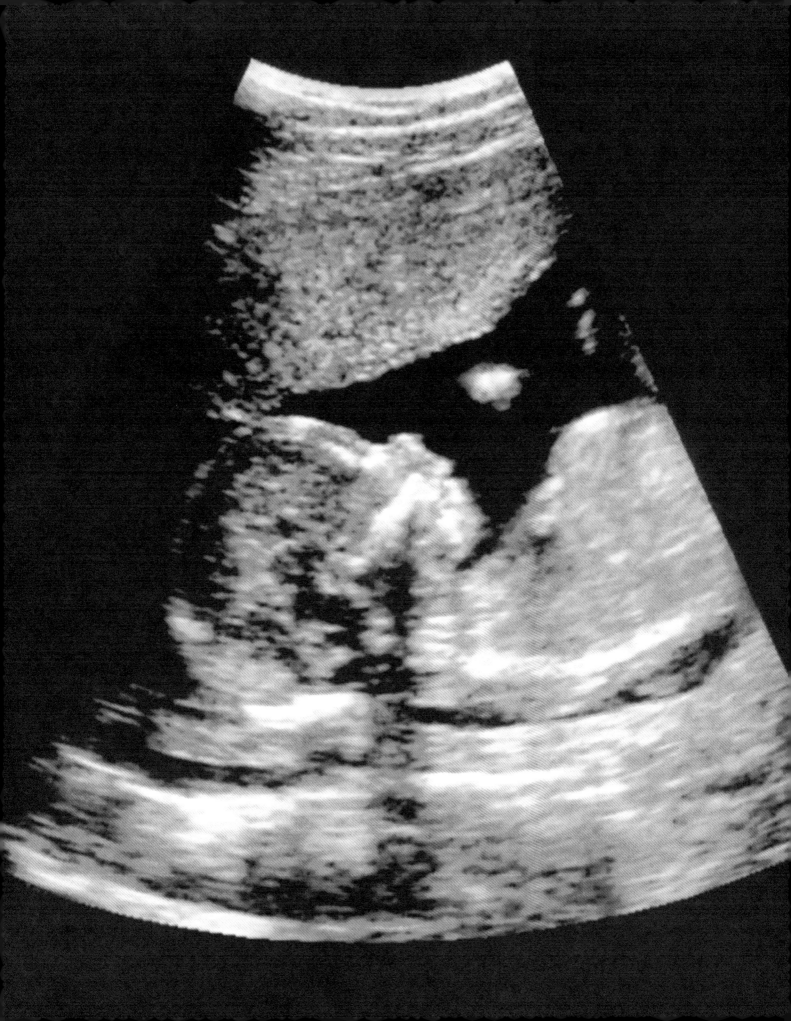

Leap

A couple leaped from the south tower, hand in hand. They reached for each other and their hands met and they jumped.

Many people jumped. Perhaps hundreds. No one knows. They struck the pavement with such force that there was a pink mist in the air.

The mayor reported the mist.

A kindergarten boy who saw people falling in flames told his teacher that the birds were on fire. She ran with him on her shoulder out of the ashes.

Several pedestrians were killed by people falling from the sky.

A fireman was killed by a person falling from the sky.

But a man reached for a woman's hand and she reached for his hand and they leaped out the window holding hands.

Jennifer Brickhouse of New Jersey and Stuart DeHann of New York City saw this from far below.

I try to whisper prayers for the sudden dead, and the harrowed families of the dead, and the screaming souls of the murderers, but I keep coming back to his hand and her hand nestled in each other with such extraordinary ordinary succinct ancient naked stunning perfect simple ferocious love.

It is the most powerful prayer I can imagine, the most eloquent, the most graceful. It is everything that we are capable of against horror and loss and death. It is what makes me believe that we are not craven fools and charlatans to believe in God, to believe that human beings have greatness and holiness within them like seeds that open only under great fires, to believe that some unimaginable essence of who we are persists past the dissolution of what we were, to believe against such evil evidence hourly that love is why we are here.

Jennifer Brickhouse saw them holding hands, and Stuart DeHann saw them holding hands, and I hold onto that.

Last Supper

Emmet's last supper with us was lamb stew, simmered all afternoon with white beans and garlic and tomatoes and oranges, served with spinach salad and fresh-baked bread, accompanied by a red wine from Tuscany. He sang, he told stories. He kept his jacket on during dinner because he was cold, although it was a warm spring evening just after Easter. He removed his fisherman's cap during the meal but put it on again when the dishes were cleared; he was cold, cold. He sang in Gaelic, he sang in English. He sang a song about a mother's love for her children and he sang a song about a whiskey jug. He said grace to open the meal, and blessed my daughter after the meal, placing on her head the same huge hand that had baptized my sons two years before at the very same table, the boys cupped in that gentle slab like fish in a sweet net.

He was very sick then, chilled with the cancer that would soon kill him, with the knowledge of it eating him as he ate the lamb, and he was weak — he had toppled slowly into the ocean of ivy around my house when we arrived, and lay there for a moment like a fallen fir, smiling — but he savored his supper like a starving man, and sipped a little wine in honor of his friend Christ, as he said, and his wit was quick and his memory rich, and when he stood by the door to go, his hand engulfing the knob, he sang a last song, in Gaelic, about calling in the animals at dusk. "I came in with a song and I'll go with a song," he said, and he did.

His last Mass, at Saint Michael's Church in Portland, was packed — people standing in the aisles, children perched on the shoulders of fathers. By then Emmet could barely walk, and he had to choose between standing long enough to say Mass or standing to serve the Eucharist. He chose the Mass, summoning all the gas in his tank to hold the Body of Christ aloft one last time, the thin wafer weighing a thousand pounds. After eating the Lamb himself he sat down in his chair, and while Communion was served by others he beamed at the hundreds of people who had come to his last supper.

He died five weeks later, on a bright afternoon, called in by the Shepherd he loved so, the God he had served so long and so well with those sinewy hands and silver voice, the God he swore was Irish, for Who better to understand the people of the suffering road? And three days later he was buried in the coffin he had commissioned, of Oregon juniper from the high desert country, and so was laid to rest Michael Emmet Harrington, priest and storyteller, son of a son of County Cork, Emmet who was named for the rebel Robert Emmet, Emmet whose name meant *truth* in Hebrew.

I loved that man, admired the bone of his character and the expansive muscle of his heart, and I sing the long strength of his love, now flung abroad to all the waters and woods of the world. I say to you this morning, Emmet my friend, the Gaelic words you said to all of us so many times, pausing at a door, the knob a knot in the net of your hand: *Go mbeannai Dia thu*, God bless you, God keep you forever.

An Independant Woman

A dear friend of mine died this morning, just three hours ago, and I have not been able to stop thinking about her; and so I write her down, to pray for her, and also to try to understand her enormous dignity and character, now lost to me.

She was born rich, as rich perhaps as any child in America in 1905, but her wealth had no effect on her character, which was from the start composed of independence and bony wit. She began college but found it uninteresting and ceased attendance, against her parents' wishes. After wide travels she returned to the family manse and there was wooed by many men of means. All were rejected. Yet one man persisted in his advances, beating ceaselessly against the granite cliff of her refusal, time and again, until finally he took her third *no* and fled sadly to Europe with it in his pocket, returning to America penniless; and then one last time he asked for her hand and heart, and she said *yes*, and so, penniless, they began life in Boston.

She was not from Boston and so did not know the manners of that musty city, the labyrinthine workings of that class-conscious citizenry, but soon enough she carved a place for herself in that frozen society and became one of its queens. But never was there a less regal sovereign than Jane, who mopped blood in a hospital during the war, who took in two young artists as boarders late in life, and who was possibly the only socially prominent woman in the history of ancient Boston to have a dog-eared subway schedule and Boston Bruins season ticket in her purse.

She fought tragedy, more than her share, her husband dead too early, her sisters dying with their minds torn loose from their moorings, a dear friend frozen in a snowstorm, other friends dying by the dozens as the years passed and their ages advanced, their absence from the afternoon bridge-table the first ominous sign of their impending deaths; but Jane could not be cowed by death or life, and even when she sold the house she loved and moved into an apartment, she lived there with grace and verve and the daily *Boston Globe* and a Scotch on the rocks at dusk, and so she leaned on the structure of her habits but characteristically refused to be imprisoned by them, or by age, failing health, and the petulant expectations of others.

Her last year she spent curled in a bed, a child again, drifting in and out of a medicinal fog, dreaming her own dreams as the days and nights passed, one sliding into the other, all distinction between the two lost; and this morning she dreamed away and I am bereft, left only with my memories and an enduring sense of the grace with which she deftly wove love and independence into a life. So weave we all, with more or less success, but this morning is lost a genius of the loom, and I weep for her, and for us.

A Prayer
for Pete

The phone rings, it's an old friend, he tells me of another old friend who is dying. He's in his forties, just married, little boy, no hope, he'll be dead within a couple of years, and dying too in a most cruel fashion, piece by piece, as his body slowly fails around the bright light of his mind, leaving him trapped in the husk of what had been a wonderfully lithe body.

I try to imagine my friend inside himself, immobile in a dark crumbled castle, his mind racing — and I have to get up and get outside and go for a walk.

So what prayer do I make for Pete? What do I say for his little boy, who will lose his father before he knew him well? What do I say for his wife, who will watch her new husband die a little every day and then be left alone with their son with the same thick red hair as his father?

I don't know.

And to whom do I address these prayers? And what do I expect to happen by those prayers?

I don't know.

Do I really think that my prayers will save Pete, or cut his pain, or dilute his fear as he sees the darkness descending? Do I really think my prayers will make his wife's agony any less, or reduce the confused sadness of his little boy?

No.

But I mutter prayers anyway, form them in the cave of my mouth and speak them awkwardly into the gray wind, and watch as they are instantly shattered and splintered and whipped through the old oak trees and sent headlong into the dark river below, where they seem lost and vanished, empty gestures in a cold land.

Did they have any weight as they flew?

I don't know.

But I believe with all my heart that they mattered because I was moved to make them. I believe that the mysterious sudden impulse to pray *is* the prayer, and that the words we use for prayer are only envelopes in which to mail pain and joy, and that arguing about where prayers go, and who sorts the mail, and what unimaginable senses hear us, is foolish.

It's the urge that matters — the sudden *save us* that rises against horror, the silent *thank you* for joy. The children are safe and we sit stunned and grateful by the side of the road; the children are murdered, every boy and girl in the whole village, and we sit stunned and desperate, and bow our heads, and whisper for their souls and our sins.

So a prayer for my friend Pete, in gathering darkness; and a prayer for us all, that we are brave enough to pray, for it is an act of love, and love is why we are here.

Table Talk

Of late I have been swimming happily in the many books of Robert Louis Stevenson, who wrote hard, died young, and had the invalid's foresight to write his own epitaph. These famous lines, *Here he lies where he longed to be / Home is the sailor, home from the sea / And the hunter home from the hill*, are chiseled in stone on a hill in Samoa, and they are, it seems to me, a bit of his own fascinating voice, now stone above bone.

By all accounts Louis, as his family called him, was a remarkable talker very early on — one friend remembers first hearing his "vibrating" voice emerging from a dark corner in Edinburgh, and riveting ears for hours before the speaker revealed himself — and many who knew him insisted that his table talk was his prime genius. He was a close student of fine talk in others, a wonderful inventor of talk in his novels, and a man convinced to his dying day (which he ended talking to his wife) that talk "is the scene and instrument of friendship, the gauge of relations, the sport of life . . . there can be no fairer ambition than to excel in talk, to be affable, gay, ready, clear, and welcome."

Pondering his lost voice, I consider the extraordinary role of talk in literature, culture, politics, religion — in short, in everything. How do we know of the past but by written talk? What would we know of Socrates, Mohammed, Samuel Johnson but by their remnant voices? What do we really know of the itinerant Judean preacher Jesus Christ, after all, than a bit of his puzzling talk?

All great literature and history (and religion is both literature and history) quotes heavily from its characters. What easier and truer means is there to delineate personality and character than by what comes from the mouth? So plays are the ordered conversation of characters capering across the stage, and music what the extraordinary singer and reluctant talker Van Morrison calls "the inarticulate speech of the heart," and many novels are either long conversations or one mesmerizing voice: Joyce Cary's *The Horse's Mouth*, Samuel Beckett's *Molloy*, Laurence Sterne's *Tristram Shandy*.

Perhaps part of the reason we so love to talk is that we learn it so early; it is our first means of communication and control, and we have an affection ever after for that which has propelled us into the wider world. Think of the sea of conversation in which children are bathed before they themselves can talk. It is an incomprehensible muddle of sound, but once the code is cracked it is the means by which the world opens like a flower — "fluid, tentative, continually in further search," as Stevenson said. Even talk with a bite, as it were, is often stimulating and beneficial: There is the argument that clears the air, the short sharp speech after much provocation that in an instant empties a kettle of rage, the vulgar poetry of oaths, the sharp words that are sometimes perfect blades for slicing away fatuity.

The voice that begins as cries and whispers, moans and burbles, grows to maturity as the utterance of our innermost soul, and does not die easily; it works furiously to persist past death, forcing itself into the future in books, wills, plays, recordings, letters, memoirs, epitaphs. It is our faithful companion, our most treasured possession, the last thing we clutch as we go ungentle into the night, the last flare of our selves and souls. Thus our fascination with last words, and our powerful wish that a life might be distilled into a perfect poem spoken as the curtain falls. Or spoken in stone over bone, as over the cheerful and energetic Stevenson, now silent after a life of rich and funny talk — which is, as he said, our "chief business in this world . . . a thing to relish with all our energy, while yet we have it, and to be grateful forever."

"It is our most faithful companion, our most treasured possession, the last thing we clutch as we go ungentle into the night, the last flare of our selves and souls. Thus our fascination with last words, and our powerful wish that a life might be distilled into a perfect poem spoken as the curtain falls…"

BRIAN DOYLE

JANNA LOPEZ is a story-seeker, writer, editor and former magazine publisher living in Portland, Oregon. Magazine MakeOver is one of her professional endeavors which serves to inspire and cultivate the substance of stories. Janna is completing her first book, *Me, My Selfie & Eye*. Janna humbly thanks Brian Doyle and University of Portland for this unique opportunity to immerse the world into the stories we're so fortunate Brian captured about shared human being-ness.